SILVER BUCK

SILVER BUCK

Andrew Hoyle

PELHAM BOOKS
LONDON

First published in Great Britain by
Pelham Books Ltd
44 Bedford Square
London WC1B 3DU
1984

British Library Cataloguing in Publication Data

Hoyle, Andrew
Silver Buck.
1. Silver Buck (Race horse)
I. Title
798.4'5 SF359.5.S5

ISBN 0-7207-1521-0

Typeset by Allset Composition, London
Printed and bound in Great Britain by
Billing & Sons, Worcester

Contents

Acknowledgements

Grateful thanks to:

My wife, Pat, steadfast in her avowed intent to 'leave me to get on with it'.

Bucket's owner and number one fan, Mrs Christine Feather.

The ever co-operative Dickinson family, jockeys and stable staff.

Suzy and Paul Doyle, Barney Curley, Tommy Carmody and David Clyde – the Irish connection.

Trainers Ian Balding, Gardie Grissell and Denys Smith.

Mervyn Brock the audio tape specialist.

The kittens on the typing keys, Stephanie Brooks, Gail Newsham and Margaret Good.

List of Illustrations

Photo Credits

The author and publishers are grateful to the following for permission to reproduce copyright photographs: Provincial Press Agency numbers 5, 6, 7, 8, 10, 12, 13, 15, 16, 17; Graham Rennison numbers 11, 18, 19, 20, 21; Sport and General 1, 2, 3, 14; Wallis Photographers 9.

Foreword

By Jonjo O'Neill, the champion jockey with a record-breaking 149 winners in 1977-78, and also champion (117 winners) in 1979-80.

It must be fair to say that Silver Buck would measure up to most horses – the one and only Arkle as always an exception – we have seen performing in England or Ireland during the post-war period.

Silver Buck has certainly earned the utmost respect of yours truly. Talk about a thorn in my side! Three of the most brilliant steeplechasers I have been privileged to partner – Night Nurse, Alverton and Jack of Trumps – all had to settle for second best against Silver Buck.

At least, I can claim to have been one of the first to find out how good he was. Silver Buck was still a raw novice, competing in only his third 'chase, when I rode Alverton against him in an Embassy Premier Qualifier at Wetherby in 1978. Silver Buck may have been flattered to beat us by six lengths because it was Alverton's first race of the season. Nevertheless, it was a performance that told Tommy Carmody, me and a whole lot of others that here was a novice of exceptional ability.

The form of that race could hardly have worked out better with Silver Buck going on to beat Night Nurse in the Embassy Premier Final and Alverton giving me one of my most memorable rides when winning the Cheltenham Gold Cup. Incidentally, I have often been asked if Alverton would still have won the Gold Cup had Tied Cottage remained on his feet after the last fence. I have always believed I would have won in any event. But if you asked Tommy Carberry, I suppose he would say that the game, old warrior, Tied Cottage, would have kept pulling something out in a battle up the Cheltenham hill.

I had been out of the action after breaking my arm in a Kelso fall when Silver Buck beat Night Nurse (ridden by Ian Watkinson) at Haydock. There was a similar outcome though when I rode Night Nurse against Silver Buck in the following season's Edward Hanmer Memorial over an additional half mile on the same course. The only other runner was Border Incident, who was in touch until falling two out. Silver Buck just led us after the last, but although Night Nurse never stopped battling, his leg went on the run-in and that put paid to his chance. The injury kept him on the sidelines for the rest of the season.

Silver Buck's owner, Mrs Christine Feather, relates in the book how Tommy Carmody, Ron Barry and I arranged to travel together when going to Kempton for the King George, and how her jockey nearly got left behind at Knutsford. We should have left the beggar there! I was on the strongly fancied Irish horse, Jack of Trumps, who started favourite, and we beat everything except that blighter, Carmody, and Silver Buck. Jack of Trumps had every chance but Silver Buck was always going that little bit better after leading at the fifteenth fence.

I am convinced that Jack of Trumps would have made amends by winning the Gold Cup but for being brought down at the eighteenth. He was going very easily for me, and we were nice and handy in fifth place but Royal Mail fell and took us crashing out of the race along with him.

Whichever way you care to evaluate the performances of Night Nurse, Alverton and Jack of Trumps, the sum total of the calculations must pay tribute to Silver Buck's brilliance. His ability to keep finding that little bit extra would keep you wondering just how much he had in hand. Silver Buck was always a very hard horse to beat. I am well qualified to vouch for that!

Introduction

Silver Buck started his training build up to the 1983-84 jumping campaign with the usual big race aspirations of his connections behind him, although even the most ardent admirer of this superb steeplechaser could hardly have failed to ponder over the possibility that this might be the near-veteran's career finale. Confidence was nevertheless high in Michael Dickinson's Harewood stable that it would be a glorious twelfth birthday that this great horse celebrated on January 1st.

It was in Silver Buck's favour, and comforting for his fans, that true to the Dickinson training tradition, he had not been over raced. He had run forty times, travelling a total of 113 miles over hurdles and fences. A Rolls-Royce of a racehorse as steeplechasers go, this son of Silver Cloud had many a memorable milestone marked with victory to his credit after six seasons during which he was a visitor to nineteen different English courses. He had never raced more than eight times during a season. And he would be making a similar number of public appearances if everything went according to Michael Dickinson's planning until the spring of 1984.

There had been talk of Silver Buck retiring after he could finish only a well beaten fourth in the 1983 Cheltenham Gold Cup. But his owner, Mrs Christine Feather, said that the matter had never been given really serious consideration. Even in his disappointing defeat, Silver Buck was making racing history by playing his part in Michael Dickinson's total domination of the Gold Cup.

It must be doubtful whether any trainer will ever again saddle five Gold Cup runners – let alone see them fill the first five places! After the brilliant Bregawn had led the Harewood team home, Michael admitted that he had been worried sick since Christmas and had lost a stone in weight. In the previous year's Gold Cup he had *only* the first two to bother about when Silver Buck beat Bregawn.

If anyone involved in the 1982-83 National Hunt season had earned a few weeks mid-summer rest it was workaholic Michael Dickinson. Before flying off to spend a holiday (a working one, of course) with American trainer, Charlie Whittingham, he was already looking forward to, and plotting and preparing for, the next season and confidently predicting that Silver Buck would take some beating in his chosen races.

No doubt, any jumping trainer worth his salt would envy Michael the problems and pressures of supervising such fine steeplechasers as the Gold Cup quintet of Bregawn, Captain John, Wayward Lad, Silver Buck and Ashley House, along with so many other talented Harewood team members. How could one man be blessed with so much horse-power to his elbow? Many trainers would give their right arm to handle just one top-notcher like Silver Buck during a lifetime on the Turf.

Michael's switch to flat racing means that he will be rubbing shoulders in competition with such notable exponents of their art as Henry Cecil, Dick Hern and Michael Stoute as his training expertise is turned to the quest of seeking more classic winners for Robert Sangster.

Of course, training a great racehorse means endless hours of toil before there can be any basking in reflected glory.

The story of Silver Buck, whose twenty-nine wins worth £159,267 made him the jumping game's record prize money earner, embraces that toil and glory, along with the inevitable tears, and above all the abundant fun that this most popular racehorse has brought to so many people.

1 Irish Days

Silver Buck is a son of Silver Cloud and out of Choice Archlesse, by Archive. Silver Cloud was foaled in 1959 and raced in the colours – maroon, white striped sleeves and quartered cap – of his breeder, Jockey Club member, the late Mr Tom Blackwell. Brolly, by Precipitation, the dam of Silver Cloud, was also bred by Mr Blackwell, for whom she won the Cheshire Oaks.

Silver Cloud's sire, Aureole, chased home Gordon Richards' first Derby winner, Pinza, and went on to finish third in the St Leger, won by Premonition from Northern Light II. As a four-year-old (in 1954), Aureole won the Hardwicke Stakes at Royal Ascot.

When Silver Cloud went into training with Jack Jarvis, at Newmarket, he was asked to race only twice as a two-year-old. He made a promising start to his racing career at Ascot in September, taking third place behind Catchpole and Peacock Throne – the first two ridden by Doug and Eph Smith – in the Clarence House Stakes. Eddie Larkin partnered Silver Cloud in the debut run and was also on board when the colt returned to Ascot the following month and finished down the field in the Duke of Edinburgh Stakes won by Hethersett. Ron Hutchinson, who took over from Larkin as the Jarvis stable jockey, rode Silver Cloud to victory in the 1962 Chester Vase. The colt's two other wins as a three-year-old came in Ascot's Cumberland Lodge Stakes when ridden by Eph Smith, and in Newmarket's Princess of Wales' Stakes with Hutchinson back in the saddle. The three victories were gained over 1½ miles but he did not seem to stay 1¾ miles when contesting the St Leger, Jockey Club Stakes and Ebor.

Silver Cloud continued to race until the end of the 1964 season, winning the Scarbrough Stakes at Doncaster as a four-year-old, and taking Yarmouth's Ben Truman Cup under top-weight of 9st 10 lb at the age of five.

Earlier in his final season, he had turned in possibly a career best effort when a two lengths second to front-running Tacitus in the Westbury Stakes, at Sandown. He was eight lengths ahead of Faberge II, who had run French-trained Baldric II to a couple of lengths in a twenty-seven-strong field for the 2,000 Guineas.

Silver Cloud was retired to stud in Berkshire, where he performed stallion duties until 1972, when a syndicate sold him to Mr David Clyde, a veterinary surgeon and owner of The Craigs Stud, at Ballyclare, in Co. Antrim. The horse died of heart degeneration in 1979 at the age of nineteen.

The deal that took Silver Cloud to Ireland was negotiated on David Clyde's behalf by trainer Peter Calver, then based in Berkshire but subsequently to move north and take over a yard at Ripon. David Clyde has often wondered whether he ought to have cashed in on a successful spell enjoyed by Silver Cloud's offspring shortly after he acquired him.

'He had six individual winners the season after I bought him, and I could certainly have done a deal that would have brought me a quick and handsome profit.'

It was after Silver Cloud became resident at The Craig Stud that Mrs Samuel Booth, of Muckamore, Co. Antrim, decided to mate her mare, Choice Archlesse with him.

Mrs Booth had earlier sent Choice Archlesse over to England to be trained by Denys Smith, at Bishop Auckland, who recalled:

'The mare was only moderate, but I managed to win a minor hurdle with her at Cartmel. I think that Mrs Booth was happy to win a small race with Choice Archlesse as a boost to stud value.'

Mrs Booth sent Choice Archlesse to Silver Cloud on three occasions. Silver Buck was the result of the first mating, and Choice Archlesse then produced a full brother, to be named Watch Closely Now, and a filly, Eadie's Choice. Sadly, Mrs

Booth's death followed not long after that of Silver Cloud.

David Clyde remembers very clearly that Watch Closely Now was a much better looking animal as a young horse than his full brother.

'But it turned out that he didn't possess anything like the same ability on the track. In fact, Watch Closely Now was once sold for beef, but he was put back into training and won a hunter 'chase. The third foal, Eadie's Choice, was only small, but she won point-to-points before becoming a brood mare.'

Silver Buck was sold by Mrs Booth as an unbroken three-year-old to Mr Brian Bamber, of Ballymena, who resold him a few months later at Ballsbridge for 1,000 gns.

In that year, 1975, another of Silver Cloud's best race-course representatives, Son of Silver (out of the Premonition mare, Now What), was running with distinction in France as a four-year-old. Lester Piggott rode Son of Silver to a three-quarters of a length victory over Lady Beaverbrook's brilliant and tremendously popular gelding, Boldboy, in the Prix Messidor, at Maisons-Laffitte, in July.

In the previous month, the same partnership had run Mr Daniel Wildenstein's mighty mare Allez France (then a five-year-old) and Yves Saint-Martin to two-and-a-half lengths in the Prix Dollar at Longchamp.

A year earlier, the family connection with Chester had been maintained by Silver Cloud's full brother, Jupiter Pluvius who, trained by Bruce Hobbs and ridden by his South African stable jockey, John Gorton, carried the Blackwell colours to a two lengths triumph over Imperial Prince in the Chester Vase.

Angels Two, a Bill Elsey-trained daughter of Silver Cloud, failed in Chester's Dee Stakes, but Eddie Hide had partnered her to a six lengths success in the Ladbroke Nell Gwyn Stakes at Newmarket.

I doubt if anyone would have been imaginative enough to predict during the early part of the seventies that Silver Cloud's son by Choice Archlesse would one day put his parents in the record books as the producers of a Cheltenham Gold Cup winner.

While Silver Cloud was undoubtedly capable of implanting the class, who could have expected the requisite jumping prowess to be supplied by a mare who was no more than a modest Cartmel winner? It is obvious that neither the breeder, Mrs Booth, nor the first owner, Mr Bamber, had any such aspirations for the horse.

It was when Mr Bamber sent his purchase to Ballsbridge in a bid for quick profit that the as yet unbroken three-year-old entered the world of the racing family Doyle. And if the Doyles ever had a dull moment after that it was never when the young horse they were eventually to name Silver Buck was around. Suzy Doyle has a tale to tell of those hectic yet happy days, and given a free rein, how well she relates it.

'Silver Buck was bought twice by J. T. (Jack) Doyle, both times at Ballsbridge – once as an unbroken three-year-old and then as a broken four-year-old. The first client found him too headstrong and unmanageable, and the second turned out to be an over-optimistic Englishman. The price having undergone a reduction 'twixt cup and lip.

'The second time around, there was a hitch up over transportation due either to the lack of it, shortage of funds, bad weather on the Irish Sea, or a strike . . . so the horse went back to J. T.'s Shankhill yard to await developments.

'Jack's training son, Paul, had moved away recently to The Curragh so Peter Doyle, family accountant at that stage, and Consil Doyle managed any horses that passed through the yard. The new horse's departure to England was showing no signs of imminence . . . nor was the expected salutary cheque.

'Peter, feeling a latent urge to conquer horseflesh other than in a financial capacity, decided that his rather weak-looking but definitely handsome brown horse was the very article for a gent's hack. So one nice crisp, autumn morning he sallied forth with a set of tack and put it on the new horse, who stood like a lamb and appeared to be frightfully co-operative.

'Peter, fortunately for him, had forgotten his hat and went off to fetch it. On his return he heard the most horrific noises . . . crashing, smashing alarming sorts of noises! Result – no hack and no tack!

'So the horse stayed in Shankhill and had to be broken, which took a long time and a great deal of patience. Paul, his father Jack, and Peter all had a hand in it. He had all sorts of idiosyncrasies and refused to be led on the near-side. In order to be lunged at all, he had to be led around from the off-side at the end of the lunge-line. He had no intention of submitting to being ridden and eventually it was suggested by Paul that some kind of deprivation was probably going to be the most successful and least aggressive means of overcoming his hang-up.

'The plan, an ancient Irish method, "a big bit in his mouth and a little bit in his belly", was put into action. And after a few days with very light rations and plenty of lunging the horse, despite himself, began to feel much more co-operative and tractable and the worst problems were over with him.

'At this stage no one really thought of him as being a racehorse, so Peter's sister-in-law, Katy, began schooling him – circles, figures of eight, etc – and trotting him over poles. He revealed great aptitude and was shown to several people as a potential show-jumper. Katy brought him out hunting with the Bray Harriers and he really began to enjoy life.

'There was a point-to-pointer at Shankhill called Great Ben who had won a couple of races. Peter one day brought the brown horse for a gallop with Great Ben just to keep the older horse company. They set off up the slope with Peter expecting his horse to be left well in the rear. To his amazement, however, he was soon far in the lead without having encouraged his mount at all! The horse found himself very quickly – with the name of Silver Buck – en route for The Curragh and with a fresh purpose in life.

'Noel O'Toole (Paul's claiming jump jockey), knowing a gift horse when he saw one, immediately took charge of the horse and the horse similarly took to him. Paul was delighted with his new animal although he realised that he was going to have to organise a very careful training programme for such an obviously sensitive personality.

'However, Silver Buck made good progress and seemed to get fit on a minimum amount of work. He was still a little odd and would not allow himself to be held, for example when Noel wanted a leg-up. Not a problem though, as Noel would just lead him off towards the gallops and jump up quietly somewhere along the way. Silver Buck's introduction to 'chase fences was memorable. As is usual, he was walked up to the first fence for a sniff and an exploratory nibble. He did stand and lower his head for a second, right enough, but he then leapt straight into the air rather like a deer over a wire fence – firing his jockey way out of the side door! But schooling progressed smoothly and effortlessly after that.

'The next step was to introduce him to the race track and Paul decided that the best programme would be to head for a few point-to-points first, rather than hotting him up with two mile "bumper" races.

'His first outing was to Oldcastle in County Meath, where the pilot was to be Timmy Jones. I was feeling cold, lazy and pregnant, so I had elected to watch the race from a good vantage point on the hill. Anyone who has attended a few Irish point-to-points on wind-swept countryside with a mist lightly caressing all one's extremities, will appreciate the advantages of a warm jeep. If the jeep is well supplied with the where with all for "hot toddies" one will also have inner warmth and plenty of good company.

'However, I was awaiting Silver Buck's debut for ages. The race was ten minutes late and I was getting very impatient. It then transpired that the entire cause of the delay was . . . Silver Buck.

'First of all he had refused to let Timmy Jones onto his back in the ring. Secondly, having then been led onto the track, he had allowed Timmy up, but then decided that racing silks were too much, so he fired both himself and his jockey into a wire fence which between them, they had pulled right across the track.

'Both the horse and pilot were eventually extricated, a bit torn, but relatively unscathed, and Silver Buck was withdrawn from the race. Timmy Jones' father did mention in passing to Paul that whereas he had no objection himself to a person giving a horse a "school" on the course he did feel that breaking a horse on the track was a bit too much.

'The other memorable happening of that day was the commentator (from his stand on a farm wagon) asking Paul to lep up and make out with his 6ft 6in advantage: "Where the hell has the favourite gone?" All Paul was able to establish was that the favourite had indeed vanished behind a tree on the far side of the track. The horse was believed to have been loaded at high speed and transported through a gateway.

'Silver Buck's next outing was much more of a routine occasion. He had had lots of practice with the colours, and he took part in the race, led most of the way and finished third, which was extremely satisfactory. Martin Brassil rode him on that occasion as Timmy Jones had had a fall in the race before. After that, we headed for Gowran Park and the Kilkenny point-to-point, where he won a distance in the hands of Timmy Jones.

'At this stage things were going very smoothly although they came slightly unstuck at Naas, the South County point-to-point, where a hunt servant's horse, trying to control the crowd, accidentally bumped into Silver Buck on the run-in. He still got up to be beaten only a neck by a horse of John Mulhearn's called Chet's Dream.

'The next win was a dramatic occasion for all of us. I had been very ill and was convalescing at home in Somerset. Paul, who had saddled a runner at Liverpool, visited me and then set off back to Ireland with high hopes for the next day. But his optimism suffered a severe setback when on the road home he had a bad car crash.

'On Sunday morning, instead of getting ready for the races, he was in the "eye and ear" hospital in Dublin preparing for a serious operation to remove fragments of glass from both eyes. The eye specialist told Paul quite plainly that he could not promise to save his sight but would do his best. Paul's reaction to that, being a Doyle (for whose specific use there cannot be any doubt that Mr Bell must have made his invention) was to take immediate recourse to the 'phone.

'Seeing, or rather thinking, that funds were definitely going to be of a very high priority, he decided to organise a substantial "punt". Having done that, he went off to the operating theatre, and all went well – thanks to a whizz-kid specialist named Louis Collumn and a horse called Silver Buck. Both man and beast then went "out to grass" for a while.

'Having spent the summer down at Mr and Mrs Jack O'Connor's farm in Tipperary, Silver Buck came back looking marvellous and it took him only a short time to get fit again. Everyone had high hopes including Noel O'Toole, who was anticipating a few nice winning rides over hurdles.

'Paul decided to give him a good piece of work. Liam Brennan had a lot of jumping horses at the time so it was planned to team up with him for the gallop. We were all then rather disappointed with the work as Silver Buck had to try quite hard and still finished a furlong behind the other horse. We consoled ourselves with the fact that our horse was not totally ready yet.

'A month later, we took the horse to Clonmel for a "bumper", his first outing on a racecourse under rules. True to form he decided to change his mind about allowing a jockey on his back. He deposited Column Magnier straight down onto the ring and wouldn't allow him near again. Mr Marsh, the stipendiary steward at that time, asked me rather dryly if the horse had actually been broken. Whilst I went into explanations about his point-to-point career, Noel, who had been leading him around, wearing a long coat to keep out the rain, had jumped up on his back – long coat and all, no trouble!

'So he rode the horse out onto the track and as he jumped down from the wrong side Paul legged Column up the other side and let the horse off straight away. Column hung on tight, gathered everything up on the way to the start, and Silver Buck then proceeded to win the race with the greatest of ease and with eight lengths to spare.

'Three days later he was sold and poor Noel went into a

state of withdrawal and near emigration (though fortunately he is still with us). Paul, who described Silver Buck as "a light greyhound type of horse with a superb heartbeat," is always a seller, never a man to refuse a good profit. So Barney Curley became the new owner of Silver Buck.

2 Catterick Coup

When the shrewd Irish horse player Barney Curley had a strong fancy he would literally put his house on it! The biggest and most innovative of Barney's many gigantic punts was the gamble he took with his Middleton Park mansion – former residence of the Boyd-Rochforts – at Castletown-Geoghegan, County Westmeath. No bothering with estate agents for Barney! He proceeded to arrange possibly the world's greatest ever raffle, and provided that two thousand tickets (at two hundred punts apiece) were sold, the draw for the Middleton Park mansion would go ahead. The minimum target was duly met and the draw took place on January 31, 1984.

Barney rates his biggest win a £350,000 touch that he pulled off with an Irish starting price job. He admits to his disasters, as when he opposed Golden Fleece in the 1982 Epsom Derby. And when he stood to win around £150,000 on Nureyev in the 1980 2,000 Guineas. Barney left the Newmarket course believing his Nureyev bet had been landed, but heard later from another punter while in the toilets at Heathrow Airport that the French horse had suffered disqualification. No one was more impressed by the bearded Barney's track record than Michael Dickinson, who was delighted to buy Silver Buck from him.

Silver Buck arrived at Tony Dickinson's Gisburn stable in the summer of 1977, and I was introduced to the horse during an autumn tour of the yard.

At that time there was nothing to suggest that Silver Buck would achieve steeplechasing acclaim as the best of the post-war era – Arkle apart! Michael Dickinson, my Gisburn guide, didn't linger long at Silver Buck's box. He just muttered something about the horse having come over from Ireland and that he would be starting the season as a novice hurdler.

Some six successful years later, Michael recalled: 'Our first impression of Silver Buck was that he was a little bit small. But after we had given him a few canters we liked him. He was very, very nervous, especially when his rider was jumping on or off him. Once you were on him he wasn't too bad, although he was a bit of a darter. He would dart off the gallops at Gisburn and canter round the fields.

'He was a very spooky horse. He would spook at everything and when he was out on the road, he had to walk right down the middle. He would be frightened that something was going to jump out of both hedges. It was infuriating for motorists, but we couldn't do anything about it.

'When we schooled him over hurdles he was desperately careful for a long time. He was so windy that we had to give him a fair amount of schooling to instil some confidence into him.'

Consequently, it was with reservations that Michael approached the task of sorting out a suitable race for Silver Buck's first English excursion. The contest that Michael eventually came up with was the two miles Ambleside Novices' Hurdle staged at Carlisle's mid-November meeting.

Michael explained: 'We knew two miles would be too short for him because he had won a couple of point-to-points in Ireland. And basically he wasn't a two-miler. But I didn't fancy him going over three miles. He pulled so very hard and I was worried that over a longer distance I would end up making the running. Once in front he would be spooking, because he had been like that whether on the roads, cantering or schooling. I figured that in a two mile race they would go a faster gallop and I would be able to settle him at the back. Over a longer distance, he would be able to pull his way to the front, and that could make life hell for me. So we opted for the Carlisle race.'

With a dozen runners going to the post, Michael had every hope of keeping Silver Buck well covered up. He was anxious not to get him near the wings of the hurdles, and planned to aim him at the middle of each flight. Silver Buck was little fancied in the betting, starting at 12-1 with the market led by Stay Quiet (2-1) followed by Mister Geoffrey (3-1).

Michael regarded his task as very much a get round job.

'He was very nervous, and I took the precaution of ensuring he had a lead going down to the start. Fortunately, the race was run at a good gallop and I was able to settle him. He jumped the first hurdle all right, but then ran about a bit at the second. He didn't quite know what to do and tried to run out. He never really got within striking distance of the leaders, but towards the last two or three hurdles, he became noticeably braver, and was running on.

'All told though, he was a pretty hairy ride that first time, and had he managed to pull his way to the front I think he would have shit himself.'

Silver Buck was only eighth to finish behind Mister Geoffrey but his first English lesson – over a trip too short and on ground too soft for such a good mover – had been an invaluable part of his education.

In planning Silver Buck's next race, Michael was faced with the difficult task of finding a three mile hurdle that was unlikely to be staged on soft going. If the ground is not frozen rock hard during December it is usually pretty soft. But that might not necessarily be the case at Catterick. There was a three mile hurdle coming up at the Yorkshire venue, where the course is well-drained, and even at the wettest of times the turf never gets really holding. It was an amateur race but there were few other suitable opportunities to be found. There are not many three mile hurdles for novices nowadays, but at at time there were even fewer.

The big doubt was whether Silver Buck could be considered an amateur's ride. The Dickinsons were worried, but decided to take the chance. Finding a jockey was no problem, the mount automatically going to Michael's brother-in-law, Thomas Tate. Thomas and his wife Hazel have been no strangers to success with their own small team of horses, stabled at Otley, a few miles down the road from Harewood.

When Michael asked him to ride Silver Buck, Thomas could never have guessed he was teaming up with a future great. Neither was he aware that the Dickinsons were keeping their fingers crossed that the spooky horse would not give him a hard time.

Michael recalls: 'I had probably held the theory before the race that had Thomas been allowed to ride Silver Buck at home the horse would have frightened him to pieces. On the day of the Catterick meeting, I would be at Chepstow partnering Big Ben, so I gave him his instructions in advance.

'I told Thomas that under no circumstances should he hit the front before the last flight. And to come right up the middle of the course, so that nothing could spook him near the rails.'

When Silver Buck was sold to the Dickinsons a condition of the deal had been that they would let Barney Curley know the first time the horse was fancied to win. Before the Catterick race, Barney got the message from Michael: 'He's a good horse, and has done one or two nice gallops. He will win provided he doesn't do anything stupid.'

Barney must have been in the front line when they handed out the luck of the Irish, because Michael couldn't have planned the Catterick coup race better with a crystal ball.

The contest had a hot favourite in Yellow Fire, an odds-on chance in the newspaper betting forecasts. This meant that Silver Buck, who had done nothing to excite interest among the betting public, was sure to open up at a good price. Not that the tipsters and punters were the only ones fancying Yellow Fire, a runaway winner of a two-and-a-half miles hurdle at Newcastle just over a week before. The Pat Rohan-trained gelding had been partnered by American amateur George Sloan when scoring with a dozen lengths to spare at Gosforth. After winning so convincingly in testing conditions, the extra half mile of the Catterick race – on an easier track and good ground – was not expected to cause Yellow Fire any problems. George Sloan, making an all-out attempt to become the first American to win Britain's amateur jockeys' championship, had every reason to believe that

Yellow Fire would assist his cause with another success.

Sloan was based at Josh Gifford's Findon stable in Sussex but had just returned from a quick business trip across the Atlantic before he travelled to Yorkshire, for what he thought was a winning ride. Punters on and off the Catterick course were of a similar mind and they confidently plunged on Yellow Fire to make him a 2-1 on chance.

Few, apart from the Dickinsons and Barney Curley, knew that the field of thirteen for the Brompton Amateur Riders' Novices' Hurdle (Division II) included a real dark horse in the form of the brown gelding Silver Buck. The Catterick bookies offered Silver Buck at 12-1 when the betting opened up, but by the time the runners were on their way in the three miles, three hundred yards, event, the odds had been slashed to 5-1.

Barney had obviously been busy in Ireland, and with other astute punters following the lead, a gamble on Silver Buck had snowballed. All that was now required for the best laid plans of the Dickinsons to come to fruition on a chilly December day at Catterick was for Silver Buck to leave Yellow Fire out in the cold.

Things went well for the first half of the race, but in the light of Michael's explicit instructions to Thomas, there was an anxious moment for all concerned when the pace-forcing Friendly Boy folded up rapidly at the fourth hurdle from home. Silver Buck was travelling so well that he had nosed his way to the front at the next flight.

Fortunately for both Thomas's peace of mind and Michael's blood pressure, along came Yellow Fire to take up the running at the second last. But just as quickly as George Sloan and the favourite's supporters might have begun to fancy their chances, Yellow Fire's finishing run fizzled out like a damp squib. Silver Buck was upsides at the last, but, as feared, he began to look about a bit, and threatened to duck going into it.

Thomas could hear Michael's instructions echoing: 'Don't come too soon.'

Silver Buck's speed on the flat took him a couple of

lengths clear, but as Michael had dreaded, he idled in front and started to pull himself up. However, he did keep going well enough to hold off the staying-on pair, Dunmarc and Wrekin Pursuit, finally putting paid to all the anxiety by winning with a length to spare.

Michael was delighted – and more than a little relieved – that 'the conditions of the sale when we bought him from Barney Curley had worked out satisfactorily for all concerned'. Barney was not saying how much of a battering he gave the bookies, but a wink was as good as a nod when he remarked: 'I did very nicely out of it'. There was also confirmation of Barney's successful coup a few days after the race as reports filtered through from Ireland that the bookies had been hit in a big way.

The Catterick setback to George Sloan's championship hopes turned out to be only temporary. His title-chasing mission had been accomplished by the time the Josh Gifford-trained Crofter gave him his twenty-third success when winning a 'chase at Stratford on the final day of the season.

3 Michael Bows Out

Michael was back on board for Silver Buck's next race, a three mile Philip Cornes Novice Hurdle Qualifier at Worcester.

'They went a good gallop and I had a super ride on him this time. He jumped marvellously, much better than in his first novice hurdle. I brought him right up the middle of the course, just as I had done at Carlisle and instructed Thomas to do at Catterick. We jumped the last hurdle just ahead of Padski, who made a mistake, and we went on to win by two lengths. I was very pleased because he gave me the impression that he had a lot more left in the tank.'

The next stop was Leicester, where Silver Buck duly completed a hat-trick, but without giving Michael the same sort of satisfaction. Silver Buck was renewing rivalry with Wrekin Pursuit, who had been just over a length behind him at Catterick and now had the substantial weight pull of 19lb.

The punters supporting 3-1 chance Wrekin Pursuit to turn the tables could not have been aware that Silver Buck had been pulling himself up on the Catterick run-in. Attracting even more attention in the betting on the Nomad Novices' Hurdle was the Fred Winter-trained Mauritius, backed from 5-2 to become marginal favourite at 13-8, with Silver Buck at 7-4.

The previous form of Mauritius was nothing to write home about but Michael points out that 'Winter was a much bigger name in racing than Dickinson at that time'.

Although Silver Buck won, the way that he struggled to overcome John Francome's mount seemed to indicate that he was not liking the ground. Silver Buck and Mauritius had the race between them from two out after Wrekin Pursuit had weakened. Francome turned out to be doing Michael a favour when he pushed Mauritius ahead at the last. It was then that Michael sensed he had things sewn up.

'He started to give me a better feel, so I just gave him a kick in the belly and away he went to win. But he hadn't been at all impressive, and the soft going must have been the reason.

'At least, he had won three novice hurdles, and I thought that was great. If they all did that it would not be so bad. On my way home from Leicester I was thinking that he might be pushed to win again because of the penalties he had incurred in novice events. However, I was pleased that he seemed likely to make a 'chaser for the following season.

'Then I thought he might be better than an average novice hurdler, and we looked around to see if there were any more suitable races for him. It was decided that he should take his chance in the Bristol Novices' Handicap Hurdle, at Haydock Park, which was our local track.

'We went there, basically, because we thought the horse needed experience. He was still green and was definitely not going to be a safe conveyance in a 'chase. We would have put him away until the following season, but that would not have been teaching him anything.

'We ran him at Haydock with absolutely no thought of winning but he gave me a marvellous ride. One of the best rides that a hurdler ever gave me. He jumped super, and he wasn't spooking half as much as in his previous races. It was only a two-and-a-half mile hurdle and I thought I had better keep him up with the pace. So I jumped him up there, and kept him as handy as I could. He would pull until he got to the front, and then drop the lot. When Silver Buck hit the front it was as if he said to himself, "panic stations," then he would ease himself back. Consequently, in the Haydock race, he ran in snatches.

'He led at about four or five stages, but I didn't think he was going to win, even though he was giving me a terrific ride.

'Then when I produced him after the last hurdle he accelerated away to win really well. Considering that he was carrying 12st 7lb and conceding over two stones to the second horse, Kelso Chant, it was a fine performance. It made us realise that he was a very good horse.'

Silver Buck's weight defying success at Haydock was some solace for the Dickinsons on a day when their hopes of winning the Embassy Premier Chase Final with True Wish were dashed by Fred Winter's The Dealer, partnered by John Francome to a three lengths victory over Michael's mount.

After showing such inspired form at Haydock it was a bitter disappointment for the Dickinsons when Silver Buck was well and truly trounced at Chepstow ten days later. The Fred Rimell-trained Western Rose narrowly edged Silver Buck out of favouritism for the Persian War Novice Hurdle. Western Rose was well backed on the strength of a smart victory over Gruffandgrim in the Tolworth Hurdle at Sandown. This time he fared even worse than Silver Buck, trailing in ninth of the ten finishers behind Ballyfin Lake, who was scoring for the 'Gruffandgrim' partnership of Fred Winter and John Francome.

Silver Buck was beaten four hurdles from home, and could only plod into fourth place. Michael thought that the testing ground conditions sunk him, and the going almost certainly put the skids under Western Rose, too.

The Chepstow flop signalled a change in Silver Buck's fortunes and there was to be little more to shout about during the remainder of the season as far as he was concerned.

Allowed to take his chance in the Sun Alliance Novices' Hurdle at the Cheltenham festival, he was far from disgraced in taking fourth place in a twenty strong field, but Michael maintained it was not his true form.

'I think he was feeling a shoulder injury. He jumped several hurdles to the right, and hung to the right nearly all the way. I never held out any hope that he would win.'

The outcome of the Sun Alliance, and also of the following Cheltenham event, the Two Mile Champion Chase, was to be of special significance to the Dickinson stable in the not too distant future.

The Cotswolds were alive to the resounding cheers of the Irish as the 11-8 on Mr Kildare was roared home up the Cheltenham hill to beat the second favourite Flame Gun in the Sun Alliance. That was a one-two for the Emerald Isle, and stylish winning jockey, Tommy Carmody, proceeded to make it both a personal and Irish Cheltenham double by taking the Two Mile Champion Chase on Hilly Way. Apart from putting him on the map in England, Carmody's festival winners played a big part in influencing the Dickinsons to sign him up as stable jockey before the start of the following season. The successful jockey on Water Colour in the third race on the same Cheltenham card, the Coral Golden Hurdle Final, the Frenchie Nicholson academy product, Kevin Whyte, was also to become a member of the Dickinson team, and indeed, a partner of Silver Buck.

A veterinary examination of Silver Buck on his return home from Cheltenham revealed little wrong with him, and it was decided to rest him for a week, and then give him a gallop. After going well in the gallop he was allowed to contest the Maghull Novices' Hurdle at the Grand National meeting. But the Liverpool story was much the same as at Cheltenham, with Silver Buck hanging and jumping to the right.

Michael thought that his mount was not sound 'but we still couldn't find anything wrong with him and decided to turn him out until the following season.'

Tragically, that was to be the end of Michael's role as ultra-sympathetic and ever imaginative rider of the spooky Silver Buck. A couple of weeks after Silver Buck had gone out to enjoy a good summer picking at the Gisburn grass, Michael's riding career was brought crashing to a premature conclusion in a fall at Cartmel's Whit Saturday meeting.

Partnering his stable's seven-year-old Irish importation, Buck Me Off – the 7-4 favourite for the Priory Handicap Hurdle – Michael did not get far beyond the second flight in the two miles, seven furlongs event. In a horrific fall as his mount slipped up on the flat, he was hurled onto the hard track, suffering severe injuries to his liver and spleen. It required seven days in the intensive care unit to put him on the road to fitness, although when recovery came it was not sufficiently complete for him to resume as a jockey. Michael didn't argue with medical opinion that another bad fall could mean curtains to more than his riding career. He hadn't visualised going on for more than three or four years.

His ten seasons in the saddle had yielded three hundred and twenty-eight winners, including five at the Cheltenham festival, and he was Champion amateur in 1969-70. How terribly Michael would miss riding winners, he had been desperately keen to team up with Silver Buck again after spending a season grooming him for steeplechasing. He had been excited, too, at the prospect of partnering tearaway two-miler I'm A Driver over fences. Now he would have to settle for a job on the ground staff, assisting his father, Tony, in training these stars.

Tommy Carmody was the man chosen to take over where Michael left off. The twenty-two-year-old Irish jockey had impressed the Dickinsons with his brilliant double on Mr Kildare and Hilly Way at the 1978 Cheltenham festival. Yet it seemed rather odd that a stylish jumping jockey with a flat racing background should be succeeding Michael, whose strong suit – in the true National Hunt tradition – was in-born horsemanship.

The Dickinsons obviously believed that if Carmody could ride winners at Cheltenham he would not go far wrong. And while there may not be any substitute for experience, there was a lot to be said for Carmody having youth on his side. He had been three times champion apprentice on the flat in Ireland, with one hundred and fifty-eight flat winners in all, and another fifty-five in just over a year at the jumping game, to which he had turned after becoming sick of the endless starvation to overcome increasing weight.

When Tommy arrived at Gisburn he wasted no time in making his working terms clear to Tony Dickinson, telling his boss, that as stable jockey, he didn't expect to be under any obligation to perform menial tasks in the day-to-day running of the yard. Which more or less amounted to: 'You are not having me mucking out'. This was something new to Tony, who thought nothing of working from dawn to dusk, and would turn his hand to anything, from preparing the feed to driving the horsebox to the races. Tony saw the funny side of it though, and went around relating the tale to his friends, embellishing it with the cutting comment, 'It must be nice when you can be semi-retired at twenty-two!'

Shortly after taking up his new post, Carmody was called upon to school Silver Buck. Maybe the horse thought he needed taking down a peg or two – or so it seemed! Michael Dickinson was horrified when Silver Buck went clean through the wing of the second of three schooling fences and buried poor Tommy underneath it. The worried Michael thought: 'God, we have only had this jockey with us for three days and we have killed him.

'It was a horrible fall, and Tommy couldn't ride again for a few days. It fairly shook him. But that was Silver Buck. He was a terror then, running straight through the wing of the fence for no reason. And we had given him a lead horse.'

Silver Buck made his debut over fences in the three miles, thirty-one yards, Greystoke Novices' 'Chase at Teesside on October 31, 1978. Michael instructed Tommy: 'Whatever you do, get round, and keep to the middle of the course.'

Tommy liked staying on the inside, but Michael insisted: 'You must not go on the inside today – otherwise you'll finish up in hospital. And if possible, get a lead.'

The way the race worked out, Silver Buck was in front long before either Michael or Tommy had bargained for. But after leading at the second fence there were no anxious moments, with Silver Buck treating both the Teesside obstacles and Tommy Carmody with much more respect than in that disastrous training session at Gisburn. The opposition had been moderate, but Tommy could not have been more impressed with Silver Buck, and after further novice wins, at Stratford and Wetherby, he was already thinking that the gelding 'might go on to achieve great things'.

With a Teesside treble taking his tally to seventeen winners in three weeks – ten of them coming in a whirlwind four day spree – Tommy was certainly making a dynamic impact on the English scene.

Silver Buck was regarded as a Stratford cert, starting at 100-30 on in a field of twelve for the two and threequarter miles Adam Lindsay Gordon Novices' 'Chase. He looked to be making heavy weather of beating Merry Legs and Super Glazepta, but Michael knew that he was up to his old tricks again.

'When he went to Wetherby the next time out and slammed Alverton, a future Gold Cup winner, by six lengths in an Embassy Premier 'Chase Qualifier, it just confirmed what a dosser Silver Buck could be when he hit the front.

'Alverton may not have been one hundred per cent fit on the day because it was his first outing of the season, but he was no mug on any occasion. When Silver Buck quickened away from him it was a pretty impressive performance.

'We now had high hopes that Silver Buck might win the Embassy Premier Final at Haydock the following January. I had finished second in the race on Broncho II and we dearly wanted to win it on our local track.

'After Wetherby, we looked round for a suitable novice event to put him right for the John Haggas Memorial 'Chase, on the same course, on Boxing Day. We wanted to win this one for obvious reasons, John Haggas having been one of the first patrons of our stable.

'The week before Christmas, we sent Silver Buck to Leicester and he pleased us with an easy win in a novice 'chase. All seemed to be going according to plan until the morning of the Boxing Day race, when it chucked it down with rain and the going at Wetherby became heavy. That was that. We didn't run him.'

There was further disruption to the Dickinson plans as a freeze-up set in, and the Embassy Final had to be put back from January to Haydock's March meeting. With the weather remaining foul, Silver Buck was forced to miss several opportunities of a run. Desperate to give him a race before the postponed Embassy Final, the Dickinsons reluctantly made the decision to send him down to Windsor, just nine days prior to the big one at Haydock. It looked easy for Silver Buck, a 7-4 on chance, in a four-horse contest for the Fairlawne 'Chase. But disaster was lurking for the favourite.

The villain of the piece was Purdo, partnered by Bob Champion, the subsequent conqueror of cancer who then so heroically took the Grand National in his stride on Aldaniti. Purdo led until falling at the sixteenth fence, where he brought Silver Buck crashing to the turf along with him. The 33-1 outsider of the party, Joint Venture, ridden by John Francome, was left in a clear lead and went on to win from Ian Watkinson's mount, Prince Rock.

Fortunately, Silver Buck was none the worse for the mishap and had stayed on his feet long enough to have a good gallop. The run was just what he had needed to put him right for Haydock.

4 Race of the Century

Michael and Tommy had their heads together discussing riding tactics during the week before the big race. Night Nurse was the rival they feared. With the Haydock distance two-and-a-half miles, and Silver Buck a winner over three, Michael told Tommy to make plenty of use of his stamina. 'We knew Night Nurse had speed, having won the Champion Hurdle twice, but there was a doubt about his stamina, although it transpired that he stayed three miles really well. I wanted Tommy to make a race of it from a long way out and force the pace.

'Night Nurse did his customary front-running and I was pleased when Tommy moved Silver Buck up to take him on at the first fence in the back straight. After that the two of them just battled on and on over the last seven fences to the winning post.

'It was a magnificent scene. Most chases get exciting at the second fence from home, but the Haydock crowd was buzzing from the second fence down the back straight.

'They talk about the race of the century between Grundy and Bustino in the 1975 King George VI and Queen Elizabeth Stakes. Admittedly, that was a great battle but Silver Buck and Night Nurse went at it hammer and tongs for a mile and a quarter over seven fences.

'Every time Silver Buck jumped to the front he would stop and that gave Ian Watkinson the chance to keep Night Nurse in the fight. That's what made it such a close race. You could say that Silver Buck stage manages his own battles. Afterwards, I was more tired than the horse.'

Silver Buck had two-and-a-half lengths to spare over Night

Nurse at the post, with Bishop's Pawn a further twelve lengths away in third place. Tommy Carmody reported that he had been confident of success throughout the race. 'Silver Buck felt fantastic, and when we took Night Nurse on going down the back straight I was sure we would beat him'

Carmody immediately predicted that there would be nothing for Night Nurse in any re-match and that Silver Buck would win the King George VI 'Chase in the following season.

However, there was an anti-climax to Silver Buck's first campaign over fences when he went on to the Cheltenham festival and failed to justify favouritism in the Sun Alliance 'Chase. Michael thought that the heavy going beat him. 'I remember ringing the Cheltenham stable manager on the Sunday lunch time. He told me it was a dry day, and the going was good. He put the 'phone down, and then the heavens opened and it rained all day after that. There was more rain on the Monday, and the ground was heavy when the meeting started next day.

'Silver Buck couldn't handle the heavy going, but he did jump the Cheltenham fences really well. It is possible the race came too soon after his tussle with Night Nurse, which was only eleven days before.' Tommy said that Silver Buck had not given him a good feel at any stage of the three mile slog. Apart from being unhappy in the mud, he thought that his mount was not at his best on the day. The Sun Alliance went to Arthur Barrow's mud-larking Master Smudge, responding to an enterprising ride from Richard Hoare to win by five lengths, with Sweet September staying on well for Andy Turnell to pip Silver Buck for second place.

Now established in the top league of steeplechasers following his victory in the Embassy Premier 'Chase Final, Silver Buck started his 1979-80 season with his sights set on success in the King George VI 'Chase and the Cheltenham Gold Cup. Consequently, he seemed to be on a collision course with his star stablemate, Gay Spartan, a five lengths winner from Jack of Trumps in the previous season's King George.

Silver Buck was the quicker off the mark, winning at Wincanton and Hereford before Gay Spartan made a successful seasonal debut at Teesside. In taking Wincanton's two miles, five furlongs, Terry Biddlecombe Challenge Trophy 'Chase, Silver Buck beat the 1976 King George winner, Royal Marshall II. The victory margin was only three-quarters of a length, but Carmody won cleverly.

Silver Buck was back in action five days later in search of even easier pickings at Hereford. His three opponents in the Dewchurch 'Chase were not in the same street and he started at 11-2 on. He won comfortably from the 66-1 chance Tarot, but Tommy reported to Michael that Silver Buck had not been too happy on the track – a factor that was to have some relevance on a subsequent visit to Hereford. Silver Buck's two wins gave Gay Spartan something to follow when he returned to racecourse action later in November at Teesside. The concensus of punting opinion was that Gay Spartan might find his top-weighted task beyond him in the three miles, thirty-one yards, Sunderland Handicap 'Chase. With 12st 7lb to shoulder, he was set to concede 30lb to the fit Flashy Boy, who had beaten Bennachie in a Newcastle handicap ten days before.

At the off, they bet 13-8 Flashy Boy, 2-1 Gay Spartan. But the one that Carmody's mount had to overcome in a five-horse contest turned out to be Eborneezersdouble, the 5-2 third favourite.

If anything was predictable about Eborneezersdouble it was that he would not get round without making a mistake. True to form, he blundered at the fourth from home, but Mark Lowry stuck fast, and it was the turn of Flashy Boy to flounder at the second last and give Chris Grant an anxious moment. Gay Spartan had not exactly been giving Tommy Carmody a joy ride, either, clouting the seventh and hitting the ninth even harder. He had led from the third, but Eborneezersdouble was well within striking distance at the final obstacle.

Shrugging off a weight disadvantage of over two stones, Gay Spartan galloped on relentlessly to keep Eborneezersdouble at bay by a length. Tony Dickinson certainly deserved full marks for producing Gay Spartan fit enough to pass such a searching seasonal debut examination. Sadly, Gay Spartan's gritty success had been achieved at a very high cost to his career. He was found to have damaged a suspensory ligament during the race. After being acid-fired, he was rested until the following season. Until then there had been abundant speculation in the racing columns as to which horse Carmody would choose in a Gay Spartan and Silver Buck clash – and such an encounter had been very much on the cards, reserved as a Christmas treat for Kempton and the King George. Carmody says he would never have had a moment's doubt. 'Silver Buck would always have been my ride in preference to Gay Spartan. Don't forget, I had predicted immediately after he had beaten Night Nurse in the Embassy Premier Final that Silver Buck would win the following year's King George.

'Silver Buck was the class horse. But it was a great shame that Gay Spartan didn't get his chance in the Gold Cup. He was the right type for Cheltenham, staying on forever, and loving the soft ground, which you nearly always get at the festival.'

Tommy Carmody could hardly have paid a bigger compliment to Silver Buck than to have preferred him to Gay Spartan as a King George mount. After all, there had only been one horse in it – although sixteen contested the race – when Gay Spartan made Jack of Trumps and the rest of them look like jokers in Kempton's big 'chase.

An important target pencilled in for Silver Buck prior to the King George was Haydock's three miles Edward Hanmer Memorial Handicap Chase. Haydock regulars were entitled to expect something special from the Dickinsons' rising star after his weight-defying hurdles win and epic 'chasing victory over Night Nurse on the course. The Edward Hanmer attracted only three contestants but what an intriguing tussle it promised, with Night Nurse (Jonjo O'Neill) taking another crack at Silver Buck and Border Incident (John Francome) by no means out of the reckoning.

The Dickinsons had decided that Tommy Carmody should not be tied to any specific riding tactics – possibly explaining why Silver Buck was the early pacemaker, in stark contrast to his usual style, in a three mile race.

Border Incident pulled his way to the front at the seventh fence and held the advantage until Night Nurse headed him at the fourteenth. All three runners had a chance two out, but there Border Incident bit the dust, and once again the Haydock battle was left between Silver Buck and Night Nurse.

Carmody, confident that he would always beat Night Nurse, edged his mount back in the lead at the last, and the result then became virtually a replica of the Premier Final, with Silver Buck going on to win by one-and-a-half lengths.

Night Nurse, penalised 5lb for an Ascot success and conceding 1lb to Silver Buck, could be said to have revealed improvement, but who could estimate how much his spooky rival had in hand? With the Edward Hanmer staged almost a month before the King George, the Dickinsons wanted Silver Buck to have an interim outing.

The Last Chance Chase at Nottingham filled the bill – until Silver Buck scared away all the opposition! That was the last thing Michael wanted.

'I knew he needed a race, and there was no other suitable opportunity before Kempton. Then things nearly went wrong in the walk-over. The local TV people were there, taking a shot of him, and there was a chap on the course waiting with a camera.

'For a walk-over, all the horse has to do is go down to the last fence and canter back to the winning post. Silver Buck was half way between the last fence and the post when he saw the man with the camera, and his spooky nature being what it is, he very nearly took fright. If he had dropped Tommy we could have lost the walk-over, for without his jockey Silver Buck might have ended up in the middle of Nottingham. I suppose that would have made good television!'

5 King George Double

Mrs Christine Feather has had many a good giggle recalling how Tommy Carmody very nearly didn't get to Kempton to ride Silver Buck in the 1979 King George VI Chase.

'A friend of ours, John Lowthian, a mad keen racing fan, and a great one for ferrying jockeys around was taking Ron Barry and Jonjo O'Neill to Kempton, and they arranged to pick up Tommy at the Knutsford Service Station in Cheshire. Tommy had wanted to leave his car there, ready for him to collect on the way back, so that he could drive to Manchester Airport and catch a plane to Ireland. When they arrived at Knutsford there was no sign of Tommy. They waited, and looked around, but couldn't find him anywhere. Ron Barry said that if he didn't turn up in five minutes they would have to go.

'On the off chance, Ron decided to have a look over on the other side of the motorway. And there Tommy was, waiting to go the opposite way! It's a good job he wasn't thumbing a lift. He would have ended up in the North of Scotland rather than the South of England. They bundled him over the bridge and into the car, and you can imagine how his leg was pulled unmercifully all the way to the races.

'John Lowthian told his story to the *Daily Mirror* racing correspondent, Tim Richards, who put it in his column. John got hold of a few copies of the paper and posted one to each jockey – with the stamp on the wrong side of the envelope! Until the day Tommy went back to Ireland, I don't think he twigged the significance of the stamp.'

In the closing stages of the King George, Jonjo and big Ron could have been excused for thinking they should have left Tommy stranded on the M6 for in this particular tale of an Irishman, an Irishman, and an Irishman it was Carmody who had the last laugh!

'Silver Buck was always going well and he gave me a great ride. His jumping was fantastic. After tracking Grand Canyon, who had taken up the running from Tied Cottage, we went to the front at the fifteenth.

'He was very nervous when in front. I had to keep riding him or he would have stopped. Jack of Trumps didn't jump too well late in the race, but Jonjo's mount was never going to beat us. I knew Silver Buck had the speed for the run-in.'

The result was a one-two-three for the travelling companions, with Silver Buck beating Jack of Trumps by one-and-a-half lengths, and Border Incident and Ron Barry – a winning combination in the 1977 Embassy Premier Final – taking third place a further twenty lengths away.

Michael Dickinson maintained that Silver Buck had won the King George without being fully fit. He explained: 'With not having a race at Nottingham our plans had been upset. Silver Buck is a lazy worker and had not done much at home. He was better a week after the King George than when he actually won the race, but we had to give him a rest then before bringing him back for the Gold Cup.'

Winning Kempton's big chase in successive years was a great triumph for Tony Dickinson in his final season as trainer. Michael admits that it was a tremendous personal relief when Silver Buck returned to Kempton the following Boxing Day and continued the Dickinson domination of the coveted prize.

'It was my first season after taking over from my father, and I felt that I needed a big winner. Otherwise, there would have been plenty of people around ready to kick me in the belly and put the knife in. They would have been saying, "he's not as good as his dad!"

'All I could think was, I have won the King George, and if I never win another big race, no one can take that away from me.

Silver Buck was bouncing back to winning form after

finding the crushing weight concession of 34lb to Sunset Cristo in a Catterick handicap just too big a cross to bear.

Tommy Carmody had given Silver Buck every chance against the front-running Sunset Cristo, but without punishing him. The kindness paid off with an £18,358.75 winning dividend when Silver Buck appeared at Kempton thirteen days later.

The King George line-up of eight included two of his beaten opponents from the year before, Tied Cottage and Bachelors Hall (the 1977 winner). Diamond Edge came in for strong support, starting second favourite, at 11-4, with Silver Buck leading the market at 9-4. Old rival Night Nurse was a 4-1 chance, with the field completed by Anaglogs Daughter, Chinrullah and the 200-1 shot Tenecoon.

The gallant old warrior Tied Cottage had met more than his front-running match in Grand Canyon the year before. Kempton's flat three miles was hardly Tied Cottage's cup of tea. Attempting to run and jump the opposition into the ground at a muddy Cheltenham festival meeting was more the Irish gelding's metier. This time Tied Cottage could do no more than give chase to that remarkable mare of the Durkan brothers, Anaglogs Daughter, the mount of Tommy Carberry.

Despite one or two jumping errors, Anaglogs Daughter maintained a merry gallop and showed the way until the fifteenth fence, but Tommy Carmody had Silver Buck cruising well in contention. A good jump at the next, where Anaglogs Daughter was not fluent, took Silver Buck to the front with Night Nurse now making strong progress to tackle his old foe. Night Nurse lost some momentum with a mistake at the seventeenth, but revived his supporters' hopes by responding well to Alan Brown's rallying call at the penultimate obstacle.

Then just when the Kempton crowd and the nationwide TV audience seemed about to witness the Christmas cracker of another Silver Buck versus Night Nurse grandstand finale, the outcome was settled at the last fence. Night Nurse gave it such an almighty clout that Alan Brown had no chance of staying in the saddle. With the danger removed from that direction, Silver Buck was left to win at his leisure.

Anaglogs Daughter kept on at one pace to finish second, with Diamond Edge taking third place and Chinrullah fourth. It was ironic that Night Nurse should be the only one not to complete the course after performing so well until that costly blunder, although Tommy Carmody insisted that it made no difference to the result.

'We had the race won some way from the finish. It may have looked as though Night Nurse was in with a chance until he hit the last fence, but Silver Buck had it sewn up.

'This was one of the many times when I thought that Silver Buck was going to pull away and win by five or six lengths, then he eased off.

'He was idling in front, but had Night Nurse challenged him, he would have pulled out some more. He was not the type to win by big margins.'

The way the King George worked out, however, Carmody's mount did win it with five lengths to spare, but of course that was only by courtesy of Night Nurse's misfortune.

Silver Buck had now earned a place on the King George role of honour as a dual winner in company with such distinguished names as Halloween (1952 and 54), Mandarin (1957 and 59), Pendil (1972 and 73) and Captain Christy (1974 and 75).

Conspicuous by his absence from those twice successful in the King George is the 1965 winner, Arkle, who was going for the double in the following year's race when incurring the pedal bone injury that so sadly brought a premature end to his glorious career.

Typically, Arkle went out battling despite the broken bone, his dogged determination keeping him going until the end and taking him to within a length of Dormant at the Kempton winning post.

6 Big Race Row

After winning his first King George in 1979, Silver Buck had been given his usual New Year's rest until getting on the Gold Cup trail . . . or so it was intended. He resumed at Newbury on February 9 in the Compton 'Chase and satisfied Michael Dickinson when 'he did it all right'.

Tommy Carmody found that Silver Buck became better at coping with soft ground as he got older. The going was heavy at Newbury but Silver Buck was not too inconvenienced and saw the three miles out well to beat Stan Mellor's good 'chaser, Royal Mail, by two lengths.

The race chosen to put the final edge on Silver Buck in readiness for Cheltenham was Hereford's three miles, one furlong, Sean Graham 'Chase, staged twelve days before the Gold Cup. Michael was worried about running him because the horse's blood count was not quite right.

'The vet said that it wasn't all that low, and would do no harm for him to run. I was afraid of blowing our chance in the Gold Cup. But the vet knew that Silver Buck needed a race and he said: "You won't win the Gold Cup unless you go to Hereford. Just tell the jockey he will not be at his best, although there is nothing actually wrong with him."

'Over the years, we have had so many horses with so-called bad blood counts, and we have run them, and they have won. One wonders why we ever do any blood tests at all. For instance, on the same day that Silver Buck went to Hereford, Cavity Hunter had a low blood count but he ran right up to his best form and won the Greenall Whitley 'Chase at Haydock Park. Silver Buck did not run well, and jumped badly, but fortunately he had nothing much to beat.

The lack-lustre effort was a reminder that Silver Buck had not seemed too happy on the Hereford track when beating Tarot and three others in the Dewchurch 'Chase earlier in the season. Punters and bookmakers took the view that he could fall and still beat the Sean Graham opposition, and he looked as if he might have to do just that at some stages of the three miles, one furlong, event.

The 6-1 on chance had his backers worried when starting slowly and then kept them on tenterhooks with some slovenly jumping. After a mistake three out, he lost the lead to the 11-2 second favourite Portway Nick and the outcome was no longer a formality. But as Michael Dickinson had said, Silver Buck stage-manages his own battles and he was now in the kind of situation that could be virtually guaranteed to bring out the best in him.

Nevertheless, he had poor old Portway Nick to thank for letting him off the hook. After jumping well throughout to capitalise on Silver Buck's errors, Portway Nick made a nonsense of the one that mattered most – the last. Robert Kington must have been fancying his chance of registering a shock result in the record books until Portway Nick's one monumental blunder.

With Kington's mount losing impetus, and Silver Buck conjuring up a leap that might have been reserved specially for the occasion, the situation changed as quickly and dramatically as if one of the favourite's supporters had waved a magic wand. Certainly, more than a few sighs were heaved on Hereford racecourse as Carmody drove Silver Buck ahead on the run-in to beat the gallant Portway Nick by half-a-length.

If Michael Dickinson hardly found his Gold Cup hopes boosted by events at Hereford, he gained little consolation from Silver Buck's home gallops during the remaining twelve days before the big race.

'He did not go well in his work, and when we saw the first day of the meeting on TV, and the ground was soft, we were in two minds whether to run. We finally decided against it.'

It was a decision that left Mrs Feather fuming and Tommy Carmody close to tears. When Mrs Feather arrived at the racecourse early on the afternoon of the Gold Cup, she received a message asking her to go to the weighing room.

'I went over to the weighing room and saw Tommy Carmody there. He looked desperately upset and nearly in tears. When he had arrived at the course, someone had said to him, "I don't know what you have come for, your horse has gone home."

'I was livid. What irritated me more than anything was that the Gold Cup is the biggest race on the National Hunt Calendar and there was not one Dickinson at Cheltenham, although the horse was there.

'I was sort of shell-shocked because I could think of nothing else but Silver Buck not being able to run in the Gold Cup. When I had spoken to Michael on the phone that morning he had asked me, "Is it raining?" and I told him it was. I had no idea at that time that he was going to take the horse out.

'It was the only time I had a real row with Michael. Had he advised me not to run Silver Buck, I would have told him to take him out. But he should have been there to see what the ground was like.

'Michael said that if I had asked him to come down to the course he would have done so, straight away. Thus a lot of the blame was thrown on me.'

Tommy Carmody maintains that the horse should have been allowed to run.

'Silver Buck's withdrawal annoyed me intensely. After all, the Cheltenham Gold Cup is a once a year 'chasing classic. Anything can happen before there is another opportunity the next season. Michael should have let him take his chance.'

In defence of the Dickinsons' decision, Michael said: 'We took Silver Buck out of the Gold Cup for two reasons. One, that he was not at his best, the other that the going was too soft. Mrs Feather was staying down at Cheltenham and we couldn't get hold of her. We tried every way.' Mrs Feather did concede that the hotel in which she was staying had experienced some problems taking incoming calls and that there had been a misunderstanding on both sides.

There was some consideration given to sending Silver Buck to Liverpool – not for the Grand National of course – but it was thought best to put him away until the following season.

At least, there was consolation for all concerned in that Silver Buck had gone through the campaign undefeated, with seven wins to his credit.

7 Tony Hands Over

Before the start of the 1980-81 season, Tony Dickinson had decided that the time was opportune to hand over the training licence to thirty-year-old Michael.

The Dickinsons had now been established in their new Poplar House stables in the village of Dunkeswick, near Harewood, in West Yorkshire, for about a year. Before moving there from Gisburn, they were often referred to as a Lancashire stable. In fact, they have always been situated in the county of the White Rose. The confusion arose because Gisburn is on the Yorkshire side of the border, while nearby Clitheroe (which figured in their postal address) is in Lancashire.

In eleven seasons at Gisburn and one at his new Harewood home, Tony Dickinson had sent out 562 winners to amass prize money of over half a million pounds. Silver Buck had supplied sixteen of those successes during his three campaigns under Tony's guidance. In his last season, Tony had been leading trainer numerically, saddling ninety-four winners to finish eight ahead of his nearest rival, Fred Winter.

While Michael was now officially the trainer – but destined to be dubbed the sage, rather than the master of Harewood – no marked change in his father's lifestyle was likely to be noticeable. Tony and his wife, Monica, both leading point-to-point riders in the 1950s, would still be playing a key role in the stable's operations at Harewood and on the racecourse.

Big race plans for Silver Buck remained the same as the season before, with the principal targets the King George and Cheltenham Gold Cup. Tommy Carmody continued as stable jockey after a couple of fine seasons, in both of which he had finished runner-up for the jockeys' championship, with scores of seventy-one and eighty-six respectively. However, the Irishman now had some talented young claiming jockeys snapping at his heels, hungry for any rides that could help them gain experience and prove themselves. In the previous season, the quintet of Robert Earnshaw, Kevin Whyte, Chris Pimlott, Graham Bradley and Chris Bell had notched a half-century of winners between them.

If there was one ride that Carmody would be certain to retain though it was Silver Buck, the horse he knew so well after a fourteen-race association which had yielded twelve victories.

November 1 was Silver Buck's seasonal debut day, just as it had been the year before. Instead of going for a double in Wincanton's Terry Biddlecombe Chase, Michael left that prize at Diamond Edge's mercy and went for Worcester's two-and-a-half miles ATV Today Chase.

Silver Buck, starting at 7-4 on, duly achieved his anticipated success, but did not have things entirely his own way. When the second favourite, Tiepolino, unseated his rider at the third fence it was left to the 10-1 chance Again the Same to make a race of it with Silver Buck. It was only by three-quarters of a length that Carmody's mount got home from Again the Same who had led at the last fence, but Michael knew that Silver Buck had been up to his tricks again.

'He was lazing about in front, and just scrambled there in the end, but I thought it was a satisfactory first run.'

Tiepolino was able to take another crack at Silver Buck in the Whitelaw Gold Cup at Folkestone. Michael preferred to attend to stable duties rather than make the long journey to see his first runner at the Kent venue perform. He left the saddling in the capable hands of owner's son William Haggas.

This time, Tiepolino gave Hywel Davies a much less bumpy ride, but Tommy Carmody found Silver Buck in a most co-operative mood and looking full value for a starting price of 7-2 on. The winning margin was a comfortable couple of lengths, with Hywel having to settle for getting the best of a private battle with Bob Davies, on Havanus, for second place.

It was the turn of Havanus and Davies to have another stab at Silver Buck in Haydock's Edward Hanmer Memorial Handicap Chase. The connections of any horse opposing him on the course which was now established as his happy hunting ground could be considered extra-ambitious.

In such favourable surroundings Silver Buck looked particularly good value for his starting price of 15-8 on to beat three opponents, the line-up being completed by Royal Mail and Nimrody. It was Silver Buck at his brilliant best over Haydock's three miles, and he readily gave a stone and a half and three lengths beating to Havanus in completing an Edward Hanmer double.

That was his third race during November, and Michael thought that Silver Buck would need a mid-December run to put him right for the King George. The W. L. and Hector Christie Memorial Trophy Handicap 'Chase at Catterick was staged at an ideal time – nearly a fortnight before Kempton's big race.

After declaring the horse for Catterick, it was not one of those bouts of pessimism for which Michael had become so famous that made him wonder if he had done the right thing.

'We were very frightened of Sunset Cristo, a young, improving horse. He was absolutely thrown in at the weights and we were really worried, not only that Silver Buck might be beaten, but because he was in danger of having too hard a race with the King George coming up.'

Tom Dreaper, the trainer of wonder horse Arkle, once made the point that 'weight would stop a train'. He was reflecting on Arkle's weight-conceding defeat when unable to overcome Stalbridge Colonist at a difference of 35lb in the Hennessy Gold Cup.

Weight certainly brought about Silver Buck's downfall at Catterick. In conceding 34lb to Sunset Cristo it turned out to be just 1lb too much. Tommy Carmody felt set for an easy victory when Silver Buck coasted up to challenge the pace-forcing Sunset Cristo at the third last.

'Then I could feel the weight difference beginning to tell,

and Sunset Cristo was not giving in. He kept finding a bit more for Chris Grant and we couldn't make any further impression on the run-in.

'It had not been the ideal race for Silver Buck, with only four runners. He is better when there are plenty of horses around him. But although he was beaten, he had done his best without taking any punishment and did not have a hard race.'

Sunset Cristo's one length success completed a handicap hat-trick following a couple of easy wins at Stockton. When Ray Hawkey's horse went on to take Wetherby's Rowland Meyrick Handicap Chase – on the day that Silver Buck pulled off the King George double – it was emphasising the enormity of the task that Carmody's mount had been set at the Catterick weights.

Another boost for Silver Buck was supplied by Sunset Cristo when he went nap in Haydock's Greenall Whitley Chase, although a big danger to him had been removed when Bregawn parted company with Chris Pimlott at the first fence.

Silver Buck's first crack at the Gold Cup was preceded by a warm-up in the three miles, one furlong, Jim Ford Challenge Cup Chase at Wincanton just three weeks before the Cheltenham target. All went well, with Carmody bringing him home a comfortable three lengths ahead of Artifice after taking the lead from Master Smudge at the tenth fence.

The Wincanton win may have looked good but as a guide to Silver Buck's Gold Cup prospects it flattered to deceive. In taking third place behind the Peter Easterby trained pair, Little Owl and Night Nurse, in a Cheltenham field of fifteen he turned in a fair performance. But neither Michael Dickinson nor Tommy Carmody believed that he was really right on the day. Doubtless the punters who ensured that he started 7-2 favourite would not dispute that opinion.

Silver Buck had held out hope for his supporters until the final fence, but Tommy was not fancying his chances from two out.

'I joined the Easterby horses turning into the straight, but he was starting to tire, and I knew he was not at his best. He had raced only once since Christmas, but winning the King George must have taken a lot out of him. He had had a hard season and gave me the impression that he had gone stale.'

Silver Buck's big race fade-out saw him beaten by one-and-a-half lengths and ten by Little Owl and Night Nurse. With other Dickinson horses also disappointing at the meeting, Michael thought they may well have had a bug.

'It might be over-stating the case to say they had a virus, but they were far from bang on. Other good horses, like Wayward Lad and Badsworth Boy, failed badly in their Cheltenham races.'

However, Michael was able to put Silver Buck away for the season in the confident belief that if the horse could perform below par and still finish third in the Gold Cup the future must have plenty more success in store for him.

8 Carmody Moves On

Tommy Carmody's association with the Dickinson stable was severed before the 1981-82 season. The principal factors involved in ousting him from his Harewood post were the continued advancement of the stable's many up-and-coming young riders and Carmody's own insistence on riding with his leathers so short.

Mrs Feather was among those least surprised when Carmody went back to riding in his native Ireland, leaving Silver Buck requiring a new partner.

'Not that I had any reason to grumble about the way Tommy rode my horse. His style didn't suit everyone though and he was always under pressure for his stirrups to be put down. The owners complained, the Dickinsons complained, the Press complained.

'He looked so unbalanced, particularly when he was going flat out. If a horse made a mistake it seemed that he would have to come off. But Tommy and Silver Buck made few mistakes between them, and I can only say that Tommy never did anything wrong for me.'

Carmody's departure, after riding Silver Buck in all his seventeen successes over fences, left the way clear for local lad Robert Earnshaw to fulfil an ambition that he had always felt would elude him.

Robert, from Gargrave, joined the Dickinson stable at Gisburn straight after leaving school, and he was in his third season when Silver Buck became a member of the team. After the horse was put in his charge and a bond developed between them, it was natural – as Silver Buck romped to stardom – that he should dream of riding his pet, nicknamed 'Bucket' on the racecourse. Robert had no connection with racing whatsoever until taking his job with the Dickinsons at the age of sixteen.

'I had a couple of ponies and rode them at home. That was the limit of my experience. The first horse I did was Fine Fellow, and I was thrilled when he won a couple of races.

'When I was given Silver Buck to look after, I couldn't get near him at first. He was frightened of me, and of everybody and everything.

'He would not allow me to brush his head. I couldn't go straight up and rub him with a rubber on my hand. I had to work my hand gradually up his neck, and then maybe I could do round his ears a little bit. But for a long, long time I was unable to get hold of his ears or anything like that. He was very nervous.

'When he was in work and started racing he would settle down somewhat. But it took years of patience so that I could go and brush his head, and even then I had to work quite a while to do his ears.

'From when he first came to the stable, I rode him nearly all the time at home. But I was really thrown in at the deep end on the day that I had to school him over the fences.

'I had never ridden over fences in public, and my only experience – apart from with hurdlers – was when I schooled a couple of handicap 'chasers.

'Silver Buck was up to school for the first time over fences with Tommy Carmody riding him. I had to go half-an-hour later with two hurdlers, and I was a little bit disappointed because I wouldn't be able to see Silver Buck schooling.

'Well, when I arrived there, the wing of a fence was smashed down and Tommy was sat on the ground looking shaken. The boss just told me to get on Silver Buck and school him. Obviously, looking down at Tommy, and the demolition job that Silver Buck had done on the wing of the fence, it was a daunting prospect.

'We have three plastic fences, and three of birch, so that you can go up either section. Instead of jumping the birch fences, which he was supposed to do, being a novice, he tried to run out with me and jumped the plastic ones. The air was a little bit blue, but Tommy relieved a rather tense situation when he said: "Well at least he's jumped something".

'I have schooled him over fences many times since then, but he still doesn't like it. You would not think he was the same horse that you see on a racecourse. He likes to have a good look at the fences at home.

'Every time he canters round the all-weather gallop, and he passes the fences, he always looks at the wings. Goodness knows how many times he's been round the all-weather but he insists on looking at those wings.

'You can predict now where he will have a look. There's a barn near the all-weather, and there are a few corrugated tin sheets that flap about and he always likes to have a look there.

'Although I had always wanted to ride Silver Buck in a race I honestly didn't think that I ever would. After Tommy Carmody left, my understanding with the boss was that I would probably ride Silver Buck in his first run of the season to see how I got on with him. Then he might ask John Francome, or another of the leading jockeys to ride him in the big races. So at that time I did not envisage being on him in the Gold Cup.

'The Terry Biddlecombe 'Chase at Wincanton, won by Silver Buck in 1979, was chosen for his first outing of the season and I was to ride him. Trust me to go down with 'flu only days before the race.

'I am plagued with 'flu, and whenever I have a cold it is usually a bad one. The boss gave me three days off and sent me home, and everyone was advising me on all sorts of remedies to get me right for Wincanton.

'I was very nervous about riding Silver Buck, and by the time of the race, I don't know which was worse, the nerves or the 'flu. During the race, he felt very strong. He is so different on the course, compared with the way he peeps and ducks about when he is working at home.

'He was very keen with me, and I had to take up the

running sooner than I wanted to. He pulled his way to the front, and I feared he might start ducking around, but he was all right, and we went on to win easily.'

Michael Dickinson was pleased to see Robert enjoying a problem-free ride 'because if anything had gone wrong everyone would have tended to blame him'.

If everything went according to plan as Silver Buck slammed Brother Will and Gun Metal at odds of 6-1 on to complete a Terry Biddlecombe Chase double – and record his third win on the Wincanton course – it was the other side of the coin for the new partnership next time out at Chepstow.

The three miles Rehearsal Chase coinicided with the end of the flat season. Things certainly went very flat for Robert Earnshaw when a race that had seemed little more than a formality for Silver Buck suddenly found the great horse struggling like a selling plater with lead weights on his feet.

Robert recalls: 'I was pleased in the early part of the race. He was strong with me although he hadn't pulled his way to the front as he did at Wincanton. I was satisfied until he jumped the last fence down the back straight, and then he just stopped.

'From being confident everything suddenly turned sour. I could see John Francome on Straight Jocelyn pulling right away from me and it seemed as though it couldn't be true.

'It had all happened in a matter of strides, and when Silver Buck fell at the fifteenth fence he didn't make a mistake at all. He never touched a twig, and it was purely out of tiredness that he crumpled up on landing.

'I was shattered by the way things had gone so completely wrong and there was nothing I could have done.

'On the drive home with my wife I kept saying that I hadn't ridden a bad race. I knew there was no way it was my fault. Silver Buck had just not been right on the day.

'Thankfully, everyone was good and understanding about it. After all, it was plain to see that Silver Buck was not his true self. The week after the race, the boss was quoted in the paper as saying that Silver Buck was not right. That made me feel much better.'

9 Superb Victory

After the Chepstow flop, Michael Dickinson might well have wondered what to expect from Silver Buck when he saddled him for Haydock's Edward Hanmer Memorial 'Chase less than three weeks later. The trainer could at least take comfort from the knowledge that Silver Buck was competing on a course over which he had yet to perform other than brilliantly.

When Michael found out that John Francome would be available, he quickly snapped up his services for Silver Buck. Francome had been planning to give his mother a day out in London. 'But I would have felt a bit silly, sitting down to tea and cake after missing a winning ride in a valuable race.'

Partnering Silver Buck to complete a hat trick in the Edward Hanmer Chase turned out to be a nice piece of cake for John in his first ride for the Harewood stable.

It was Silver Buck's old foe Sunset Cristo who predictably cut out the pace over the three miles. The leader kept up a great gallop but had both Silver Buck and the Irish trained Royal Bond, ridden by Tommy Carberry, challenging him at the final fence. The other two contestants, Night Nurse and Salkeld, were well out of the reckoning. Then Royal Bond squandered his chance by coming to grief.

All that was required from Silver Buck to settle the issue was a flash of that famous acceleration. He delivered the goods, seemingly a shade grudgingly, although such an assessment of his back-to-form display might be taking something away from the game Sunset Cristo, who never gave in after he was headed and rallied to keep his margin of defeat to a respectable one-and-a-half lengths.

It was disappointing to see Night Nurse trailing in thirty lengths behind Sunset Cristo in third place. Indeed, there had been plenty of punters believing that this might be the Malton horse's big chance to put one over his arch rival, and Night Nurse was 11-8 favourite at the off, with Silver Buck 5-2, and Royal Bond 3-1.

Francome's verdict on the victory was: 'A super horse. Anyone can ride him until he hits the front. Then he needs ten men on him!'

Silver Buck had idled on the Haydock run-in, and needed a couple of cracks to make him go about his business, but Michael Dickinson was not complaining.

'It was a great relief to me that he had won after the disaster at Chepstow, and it made that race even more mysterious. We still didn't know what had gone wrong. My stable staff, and in particular Brian Powell and George Foster, deserved much of the credit for Silver Buck recovering so well.'

With Nottingham altering the conditions of the Last Chance Chase in an attempt to attract more runners, Michael was unable to find a suitable stepping stone for Silver Buck before the King George, and he would have to go to Kempton without a warm-up.

As it turned out, Silver Buck and the rest of the Kempton candidates were left out in the cold of a White Christmas. Out of the eight boxing day meetings, only Newton Abbot survived. Racing in England had been iced-up since December 17. The King George was postponed from Saturday until Monday, but Kempton remained in deep freeze over the weekend and the complete fixture was lost. Not that the abandonment had robbed Silver Buck of his hat-trick or the Dickinsons of a four-timer in the race. On the Saturday morning, Silver Buck was found to be lame. Michael was called to his box and he saw that the horse was very lame behind.

'There was a big panic after that but fortunately a veterinary examination revealed there was no bone damage. He had to be kept in his box, but when he was allowed exercise once again, we managed to get him ready for the Cox Moore Sweaters Handicap 'Chase at Market Rasen on March 6.

'He needed this race if he was to go for the Gold Cup. But he had had the absolute minimum of work. We thought that if he ran third, he would have done well.

'Robert Earnshaw was not free to partner him because he was on Bregawn in the Greenall Whitley Chase at Haydock on the same day. We decided that Kevin Whyte would ride him. It was a good opportunity for us to repay Kevin for riding Silver Buck in some of his work at Harewood.

'When Silver Buck won we were over the moon. He jumped and went well for Kevin, and to win under 12st 7lb, beating Moor Close, who was receiving a lot of weight, was far more than we could have hoped for. Only then did we think we had a chance of winning the Gold Cup.

'At no stage following the injury he sustained at Christmas until he had won at Market Rasen did we dare entertain any thoughts about the Gold Cup. It had been no more than a long shot.

'No one had done more than George Foster, who looks after our sick horses, to enable Silver Buck to get back on the racecourse before Cheltenham. In snow, frost, whatever the weather, George had never failed to see that Silver Buck received treatment for his injured foot.

'George had to give him treatment with a machine twice a day. Each session, at morning and night, lasted an hour. He would go out into the yard at 7 o'clock in the morning, or in the darkest winter night – even if there was two foot of snow – and see that Silver Buck's foot was treated on the machine. And yet George knew there was little chance of Silver Buck getting to the Gold Cup. He showed tremendous dedication to duty.

'After Silver Buck had started to canter again we used to get him out of his box each night just to make sure he was sound. We had him out one night and found that he was lame in front. We were weeks behind in our training schedule, and I remember father saying: "Well, that's it, the Gold Cup's out!"

'Fortunately, it was only a bruised foot, so he just missed a couple of days' work.

'After he had won at Market Rasen we worked him the following week and he went really well. The race had brought him on. He had needed it, and blew a lot.

'Just before Cheltenham we had his blood tested and his figures were the best they had ever been. And he looked well, too.

'About a fortnight before the Market Rasen event, the racing writer and racecourse commentator, Robin Gray, came to Harewood on a stable visit. He was staying with *Timeform* race reader, Colin Russell. He didn't say a lot when he looked at Silver Buck, but he clearly was not impressed.

'He admitted to me afterwards that he thought we were nuts to even try and get Silver Buck ready for the Gold Cup. In his view, the horse didn't look anywhere near fit. And Colin Russell was of a similar opinion.'

While Silver Buck was doing his stuff for Kevin Whyte at Market Rasen, Robert Earnshaw was experiencing mixed fortunes from his Haydock rides. Wayward Lad gave him a great start to the afternoon by making most of the running to take a prize of £12,383 in the two-and-a-half miles Timeform Chase. Few punters got rich from Wayward Lad, although he was backed from 4-7 to 2-5.

Neither did the bookies take any chances with the well handicapped Bregawn in the Greenall Whitley Chase, but the 11-10 favourite came unstuck. Robert was uneasy right from the start of the race when Bregawn dropped himself out.

'He was struggling early on, but eventually I got him running, and he made up ground to be there with a winning chance in the home straight, but then Little Bay fell and hampered us at the second last.

'By the time that Bregawn had recovered, it was too late. He finished strongly but we couldn't reach Scot Lane, who beat us by a length. He would probably have won but for being denied a clear run at that crucial stage. After my disappointing ride on Bregawn, I was glad to see that Silver Buck had made no mistake at Market Rasen.'

10 Gold Cup Glory

Robert Earnshaw was keeping his fingers crossed that he would get a ride in the Gold Cup, but he thought it was more likely to be Bregawn than Silver Buck. Robert had ridden Bregawn to two of the four victories that preceded his Haydock defeat, with Graham Bradley and John Francome the other successful jockeys.

Bregawn's failure to win the Greenall Whitley off a handicap mark of 10st 9lb (including a 7lb penalty) hardly suggested that he was in the same street as Silver Buck, who was obviously the one that Robert would want to be on at Cheltenham.

'I didn't dare think that I might get the ride, and it was only about a week before the race that I knew for definite that I would be on Silver Buck.

'I get gee'd up about any big race, and it was even more so with the Gold Cup. I tend to dream on occasions like this and usually I'm on a horse that loses by half-a-length or a short head.

'When Newmarket trainer, Jeremy Hindley, booked me for Arkan in the Daily Express Triumph Hurdle, which opens the Cheltenham programme on Gold Cup day, I thought that might help to relieve some of the tension before I rode Silver Buck.

'But I was a bag of nerves while waiting for the Triumph Hurdle, and I said to "Sooty" Whyte, who had been sharing Silver Buck's home work with me since he joined our stable, that I wouldn't mind a cigarette.

'That shows how nervous I was, because I had packed up smoking a few years before when I was really bad with 'flu.

He said he would give me a cigarette, but I had second thoughts because I knew it would start me smoking again.

'Sooty said he would be around later on if I changed my mind. And before the Gold Cup I was so nervous that I would certainly have taken a cigarette off him, but he wasn't there. I was absolutely pining for a smoke, but he never turned up.

'Once I was in the saddle, and down at the start, I was all right. And when you're out on the track during a race there is no time to be nervous.'

If Robert required pre-race sympathy, it would have readily been supplied by Mrs Feather, who regards the Gold Cup as a 'really nerve-wracking business'. Mrs Feather and her husband, Robin, had been invited to join some friends in a private box on the course, but Silver Buck's owner was finding the tension and the long wait almost unbearable.

'In an attempt to get away from it all, we walked to the racecourse stables, where the only people around were lads dealing with horses. An official on the entrance said: "You can't go in there". I told him we just wanted to stay where we were and watch.

'Robin had a race card and we checked the runners as they were led out from the stables. It was brilliant of him to think of something like that to take my mind off Silver Buck. I felt much more relaxed.

'All the Gold Cup runners looked pretty good, but I thought that Silver Buck was outstanding and what's more he was obviously racing fit. According to TV commentator Julian Wilson, Night Nurse "looked as hungry as a tiger" in the paddock. Well he didn't look hungry at all to me, indeed, I thought he was a shade fat, whereas Silver Buck wasn't carrying an ounce of extra weight. That Market Rasen race had just put him right.

'Now it was time to decide from which vantage point we were going to watch this famous race. I didn't want to go to the box, so I plumped for the owners' and trainers' stand.

'I had difficulty in finding it, and then I realised I was getting back into a daze again. It's a rotten little stand at

Cheltenham for the owners and trainers. I suppose they don't care because they get very few people using it.

'Michael Dickinson, I'll have you know, watched the race on television, in the weighing room while nice and comfortably seated.'

If Robert Earnshaw and Mrs Feather were finding the tension difficult to combat, there had been nothing in Michael Dickinson's demeanour to suggest that he was experiencing a similar problem when I saw him earlier in the day. While window-shopping in Cheltenham, a voice had boomed out behind me . . . 'Andrew' . . . and I had turned to see Michael looking for all the world – sartorial elegance apart – like a delegate heading for a San Francisco hippy convention rather than the trainer of contestants in the Gold Cup. With both arms laden with flowers, 'for the lady upstairs,' as he put it, Michael was making his way to his white Mercedes parked at the kerbside. He explained that the flowers were for Robert Dickinson's wife, Lucy. 'I always stay with them for Cheltenham so that I can have a nice, quiet time.' Declining his offer of a lift to the racecourse – my somewhat less ostentatious vehicle being secreted down a nearby side-street – I wished him good luck in the Gold Cup as his sleek, flower-bedecked conveyance sped away.

Seeing Michael reminded me of a betting 'system', based simply on superstition, that was devised by myself and a regular travelling companion, the northern racecourse owner and punter, Len Marginson. We noticed that the first trainer we saw on arriving at a racecourse usually had a winner that day. We were continually kicking ourselves for not following the system. I once took a car load of punters to Aintree on Grand National day, and the first trainer we saw was Gordon Richards. I told my companions about the system and the result was that everybody in the party backed the Richards-trained Grand National winner, Lucius . . . except me!

I must confess that Silver Buck was not my Gold Cup selection, I had begun to wonder if Cheltenham was really his scene, and even the fact that he was now the 'system' horse didn't tempt me to back him. The odds were good enough for he was offered at 9-1 in some places on the course before starting at 8-1. Night Nurse, the one I had plumped for, seemed full value for favouritism at 11-4. Reg Spencer's popular performer usually had to play second fiddle when Silver Buck was around, but he had possibly turned in his finest effort over fences when runner-up to stablemate Little Owl, with the Dickinson horse a well-beaten third, in the previous year's Gold Cup.

Whereas Silver Buck's big race preparation had been disrupted by injury, Night Nurse had enjoyed a steady build-up to Cheltenham and apart from that early-season flop in the Edward Hanmer his form was difficult to fault. I had been most impressed by the way Night Nurse slogged through the mud to outstay Captain John at a difference of 11lb in the Mandarin Chase at Newbury. Events at Cheltenham that afternoon were to emphasise the impossible handicap tasks that Night Nurse had been attempting when he was placed behind Bregawn at differentials of 19lb and 20lb respectively in Haydock's Peter Marsh 'Chase and the Freshfields Holiday 'Chase at Kempton.

Less than three weeks before the festival, Peter Easterby had sent out the eleven-year-old to turn in a very satisfactory trial at Doncaster, where his twelve lengths victory was achieved at the chief expense of Fred Winter's 1977 Gold Cup winner, Midnight Court.

However after running so inspired for most of the season and rarely failing badly at any time throughout a wonderful career over both hurdles and fences, Night Nurse was to prove a complete flop in his final bid to become the first Champion Hurdler to win the Gold Cup. On the final circuit, Jonjo O'Neill found his mount dropping right out of contention, and Night Nurse's supporters had written off their bets long before the horse was pulled up with two fences to go. Up front, Tied Cottage had been blazing his usual trail through the mud, but at fourteen years of age it was no surprise to see him come to the end of his tether before the second last. If Jonjo O'Neill on Night Nurse and Gerry Newman on the Irish horse had seen their Gold Cup hopes disappear, Robert Earnshaw was beginning to sense victory, barring any accident.

'Silver Buck had me worried three from home when he jumped the fence and nodded a little on landing. So going to the second last I gave him a little kick and said, come on now. It was like waking a sleeping giant and I wondered if I had overdone it. He got really keen with me, and I found we had raced into the lead far too soon.

'I was worried that he might start to idle, but he could hear another horse and kept going. Had anything got within striking distance of us he would have gone on again.

'At the last fence I was saying now whatever you do don't fall. He jumped it safely enough, and then I was aware there was something within a couple of lengths of us, but not too close. I felt for sure, though, that he would find anything that was required.

'It was only after passing the winning post, and when Graham Bradley had shouted to me a couple of times to offer congratulations before he came across and put his arm around me, that I realised Bregawn was the one chasing us home in second place.'

Michael was confident that Silver Buck had the race wrapped up from the moment that Robert kicked him on at the second last. 'He was cruising round that bend into the straight. He was running away, and the only question was, how far is he going to win?

'Then he started to idle and Bregawn got to within two lengths of him. He was never going to win by any more, but he was certainly not going to stop.

'Silver Buck may not have been pulling away up the Cheltenham hill in Arkle fashion, but that's not his style, and I did feel he had a lot in hand.'

As if the strain of the occasion had not been more than enough for Mrs Feather, she faced a completely different hazard as she watched the race alongside Monica Dickinson.

'Silver Buck's jumping seemed to get better and better on the second circuit and a marvellous leap virtually took him from sixth into third place.

'And how smoothly he came down that hill! He was literally lobbing along, and there was no waving of sticks, or anything like that. He jumped the third from home and plunged a little, but not a bad jump. And when he came round that bend he was going unbelievably well.

'By this time, they had all got their sticks out, and Bregawn was in second place with Graham Bradley really right down to it and riding him like the clappers.

'At that moment I was hit in the stomach by Monica Dickinson's handbag. I wasn't expecting to take a blow in the middle like that. "We are going to win" she said, and wham!

'I was slightly taken aback, but recovered when Silver Buck made a marvellous jump at the second last.

'But he made a slight mistake at the last, brushing through the top of the fence – and that was when Monica hit me again as Silver Buck landed over the fence.

'All I could see at this juncture were the two caps of the jockeys on Silver Buck and Bregawn. After the last fence I couldn't see a horse at all.

'Monica, screaming her head off, hit me again with her handbag – and then completely disappeared. I don't know where she went. She must have rushed down to where the runners come in at the gate. My hat was knocked off about three times as we fought our way into the winner's enclosure. It was just so exciting.

'Everyone seemed to be either congratulating me or asking me questions. I was requested to do a recording for radio, and they said to me: "And what do you feel like at this moment, Mrs Feather?" I said: "Wonderful!" And then when they inquired: "How long have you had the horse?" I said: "Wonderful!" In the heat of the moment it's just too exciting for words.

'I was invited to the weighing room to have drinks with the stewards, and they asked me to sign the visitors' book or whatever it is, and I couldn't hold the pen.'

Among those rushing to congratulate Mrs Feather was Silver Buck's former partner, Tommy Carmody, who could hardly have felt other than sad that he had not been in the saddle on such a momentous occasion.

He admitted: 'After my successful association with Silver Buck, including his two wins in the King George, while I was with the Dickinsons, I had to be disappointed that I couldn't be on him in the Gold Cup. And especially so after being all set to ride him in the 1980 race until he was withdrawn, and then finishing third on him in the following season. Nevertheless, I was pleased for Robert Earnshaw, who had taken his chance on Silver Buck so well.

'I think that Silver Buck's rest from racing at Christmas, and early in December, must have done him a power of good. He had enjoyed an easy time before Cheltenham, compared with other seasons. A horse has to be at his absolute best to win the Gold Cup. You cannot abuse a horse and expect it to win a 'chasing classic.'

As Robert Earnshaw was led through the jostling crowds pushing their way towards the winner's enclosure, he was still trying to convince himself that it was all really happening to him, and that it was not just a change of luck in one of his many dreams.

'I just felt numb when the race was over. Winning the Gold Cup was the ultimate for me, and I couldn't believe it. I hardly noticed the crowd was there.

'After I had taken the saddle off, Michael said: "Don't forget to weigh in." Then somebody – I can't remember who it was – took my arm and virtually sat me down on the scales.

'I had won the Amoco jockey of the month award for February, and they had said they would present me with the winner's trophy, a whip, during a race meeting. A week before the Gold Cup they rang me up and said "We'll present you with the whip at Cheltenham, and hopefully after you have ridden a winner." Of course, I had thought, there's no way I'll have a winner at Cheltenham. As things turned out, they were delighted to be able to make the presentation after I had won the Gold Cup, but before that I was rushed off for TV and radio interviews.

'There had been little time to think about anything, and all the way home I was still trying to convince myself that I had won the Gold Cup. It just had not sunk in.

'All the boys had gathered for a celebration at our Yorkshire haunt the Spacey Houses, where Charlie, the manager, had the champagne ready on ice, and we had a great time.

'Obviously, it would be wonderful to win the Gold Cup again, although it might be something of an anti-climax. Nothing could ever surpass my win on Silver Buck.'

The Gold Cup triumph had fully vindicated Michael Dickinson's unshakeable faith in Silver Buck's ability to get the Gold Cup distance despite the previous Cheltenham defeats.

'Everybody told me that he wouldn't stay, but I used to ride him, and a jockey should have a fair idea of a horse's capabilities.

'I had always been one hundred per cent sure that Silver Buck would stay the Gold Cup distance of three-and-a-quarter miles. He is bred to stay and had won a bumper and a point-to-point as a young horse. And he was winning over three miles during his novice hurdling days.

'Lord Oaksey was one of those who doubted Silver Buck's ability to stay. We had our friendly disagreements about it for three years before the Gold Cup win. Then I had my little say. It was only a joking matter but I felt it wanted putting right.

'Oaksey was so adamant that the horse wouldn't stay, but that opinion seemed to be based on very little evidence. Surely he knew, like everyone else, that Silver Buck was not at his best on heavy ground.

'The only time that Silver Buck had not stayed was at Cheltenham in the Sun Alliance 'Chase in 1979, when the going was terribly heavy and he finished third. And that race came after a tremendous Haydock duel with Night Nurse that might have taken the edge off him. I just could not see how Oaksey's opinion was based on factual evidence.

'The day after the Gold Cup we turned Silver Buck and Bregawn out in a field together for about an hour. One day they had been battling against each other up the hill in the closing stages of the Gold Cup at Cheltenham and twenty-four hours later, there they were, out in this little paddock at home, eating grass together.

'We never rode them after that. They would go out each day for about an hour until we turned them out during the summer and they became the best of mates.'

11 Another Haydock Triumph

From the very first day that Silver Buck showed his disdain for schooling over fences when dumping Tommy Carmody, he never became a reformed character on the trial ground. By the time the 1982-83 season came round Michael had given up with him rather than let the horse drive him to despair.

'He remained so bad at schooling that we just allowed him to go over the three fences once. We schooled Silver Buck and Political Pop behind another horse and they were terrible.

'Political Pop is a pretty good jumper on the racecourse, and he finished seventh in the 1983 Grand National, but if you had seen him schooling you would wonder how he could get round a point-to-point course, let alone Aintree.

'We have had plenty of bad jumpers at home who were perfectly capable on a racecourse, and we have also had the brilliant ones who were no good on the track. Apart from giving Silver Buck little schooling, we had learnt – and it was by force of circumstances – that he did not want much work.

'The older horses are, the wiser they get, and they don't exert themselves as much. So the idea is not to take Silver Buck to the gallops too often, and then when he goes he puts more into his work. What we are after is quality work, not just boring, repetitive stuff. It's no good taking him to the gallops if he is going to doss.'

Silver Buck was ready to resume at Wincanton towards the end of October, his target being to take the Terry Biddlecombe Challenge Trophy for the third time.

It was most apt that one of the only two entries not scared away in the two miles, five furlongs, 'conditions' 'chase was called Easy Pickens. The race looked a real doddle for the Harewood horse. It was an exciting week for Robert Earnshaw, looking forward to teaming up with Silver Buck again and riding Wayward Lad a couple of days later.

Robert had ridden twenty-seven winners in his Gold Cup season, six of them supplied by Wayward Lad, who was to make his season's debut in the Worcester Evening News Chase. It was a much more confident Robert, who despite finding the rather awkward journey from his Yorkshire base to Wincanton 'a bit of a bind', returned to the Somerset venue to record another victory.

Silver Buck, at 6-1 on, was a cantering winner from Easy Pickens and Regents Garden. Then it was just as easy for Robert on Wayward Lad (11-4 on), who beat Night Nurse and Gaming Dice in a three-horse contest at Worcester.

Michael wanted Silver Buck to have another race before the Edward Hanmer Memorial at Haydock on November 24, and he selected Stratford's Hawkes Bay Trophy which came an ideal thirteen days before.

The two-and-threequarter miles Stratford chase cut up into a match between Silver Buck and Gambling Prince. Michael recalls the race with a laugh, relating how Gambling Prince's owner-trainer, Mrs Gill Jones, was going round seeking everybody's advice as to how her horse could beat Silver Buck. 'I think she must have asked everyone, from the tea lady to the man selling the papers, as well as several trainers.' Mrs Feather went over to chat with Mrs Jones – 'a most delightful person' – in the paddock.

'I wasn't feeling conceited about the situation, with Silver Buck seeming to be a certainty to win. There was a fellow with Mrs Jones, and he was giving instructions to the jockey, John Burke. He said: "Now if you fall remount, remount, remount and remount again!" And when the two horses were going out onto the course, the fellow's parting shot to the jockey was: "Whatever you do, don't get boxed in".'

'The race was run in that spirit, and Silver Buck also showed he was enjoying himself by jumping every fence in fantastic style and making all the running to win by a distance.

'I take my hat off to Stratford. There was a cigarette box for the winning owner, but they didn't forget Mrs Jones, presenting her with the most beautiful bouquet of flowers for being such a good sport. I thought that was a terrific gesture and you wouldn't get that at every racecourse.'

Robert Earnshaw had been forced into making all the running when John Burke adopted the tactical ploy of taking a pull at his mount as the tapes went up.

'He was determined to make me lead in the hope that my fellow might stop and look at everything. But I was well prepared and I doubt if he would try that again. There was no chance of settling Silver Buck to stay with the other one, so I just accepted the situation and went off in front, but there were no real problems.'

Gambling Prince was well and truly trounced by Silver Buck, but there was no disgrace in his failure against a top-notcher, from whom he would have received a considerable amount of weight in a handicap.

Since winning the Northern Hurdle at Haydock Park and Newbury's Greenham Group Trophy during the 1976-77 season when trained by Mrs Jones's husband John, who was so tragically killed in a car accident, Gambling Prince had proved a stalwart over fences.

Michael was delighted by the way that Silver Buck went about his work in between Stratford and Haydock.

'He looked well and galloped well, which is very heartening because horses do get a little bit fed up of working at home. After he had been off with his injured foot in the previous season we did a lot of walking work with him up a hill. The vet thought it would be best to exercise him on grass rather than on the road, so we worked him up the hill, which is about one in five or six. That seemed to do the trick, and when we started training him for the following season we gave him a lot of walking up and down hills, and not too much galloping. A horse walking up and down a hill has got to use himself. This is the way he was prepared before he went to Haydock for the Edward Hanmer. He looked in tremendous shape and was obviously very happy in himself.'

After a couple of easy runs that amounted to little more than pipe-openers, the Haydock opposition was a lot tougher, although not much stronger in numbers. Shouldering 12st in the three miles limited handicap, Silver Buck was opposed by Royal Judgement (11st 8lb), Sunset Cristo (10-12), and the bottom weighted pair, Burrough Hill Lad and Master Smudge (10-7).

With Sunset Cristo in the line-up the contest would not lack a pace-maker, but the consensus of opinion was that Burrough Hill Lad would be the one bustling up Silver Buck at the finish. Burrough Hill Lad had started the season by beating Winning Brief and Imperial Black in Stratford's Sean Graham Chase and then reverted to two-and-a-half miles to record a resounding victory in a Lambert and Butler Qualifier at Ascot.

Respect for Burrough Hill Lad, the Edward Hanmer second favourite at 3-1, enabled Silver Buck's backers to trade at a top priced 4-5, before a single wager of £8,000 to £10,000 resulted in the course specialist shortening to 8-11 at the off.

Michael Dickinson was confident that Silver Buck would be capable of coping with the up-and-coming Burrough Hill Lad despite the 21lb weight differential.

'Jenny Pitman, never one to hide her light under a bushel, said that her improving novice would give our horse one hell of a fright. But Silver Buck gave away the weight and paralysed Burrough Hill Lad.

'They jumped the last near enough level, and then Silver Buck very quickly settled it in a matter of strides. He went three lengths clear, then idled for the rest of the way.

'His jumping was spectacular and he really stamped his authority on the race, and could not have been more impressive. He goes well for Robert Earnshaw and they have confidence in each other. That was certainly showing through.

'I said to Jenny Pitman after the race: "I've had a word with Silver Buck and he told me that he hadn't been at all afraid of Burrough Hill Lad. But I'll tell you what Jenny, I'm frightened to death of you." '

'She replied: "You're not, are you Dicky?" And I said:

"Yes I am – most men are, aren't they Jenny?" She just laughed that off.'

Robert Earnshaw confirmed that in winning the Edward Hanmer for the fourth time, Silver Buck had given him the feel of a horse in absolutely tip-top trim.

'It was a brilliant ride and he could not have jumped better. The run was as good as any I have had on Silver Buck.'

12 Lad Beats Buck

After Silver Buck's authoritative success at Haydock the leading bookies were unanimous in making him favourite for the Tote Cheltenham Gold Cup with 5-1 the best price.

His next important objective was the King George and he seemed to be bang on target for the treble attempt. Then a week after Haydock, Michael reported that Silver Buck had 'done his curb' during a canter and had pulled up lame.

'We had to blister it, and he was forced to stay in for a few days. Fortunately, he was very fit before the accident. He didn't miss too much work and when we gave him a gallop he went well. But he only had time for one good gallop and he could have done with two.

'He was not going to be as fit as he had been for the Gold Cup, but we still thought he would win the King George. It was a good race and I was afraid of Little Owl because he had beaten Bregawn handsomely at Haydock earlier in December.

'I slightly preferred Silver Buck to Wayward Lad but the yard was completely split between them. The Silver Buck clan included Robert Earnshaw and Kevin Whyte, while the head lad, Brian Powell, has always been a fan of Wayward Lad, and the two vets, Antony and Simon Stirk, took different sides. There has always been this kind of friendly rivalry in the stable.'

Michael had much more on his mind than the two King George candidates as Boxing Day approached. He was planning to send runners here, there and everywhere and the one thing that he could do without was a white Christmas. He was spared such a nightmare as mild weather enabled all

Silver Cloud (*right*), sire of Silver Buck, seen here winning the Cumberland Lodge Stakes 1962 when ridden by Eph Smith.

Brolly, Silver Cloud's dam and granddam of Silver Buck winning the Clarence House Stakes at Ascot, 1952.

Aureole, grandsire of Silver Buck, after winning the Coronation Cup, Epsom 1954.

Silver Buck's first win — Clonmel 1977 with Mr C. P. Magnier up.

Silver Buck ridden by Michael Dickinson leads from Kelso Chant (A. Harrison) to go on to win the Bristol Novices' Handicap Hurdle, January 1978.

Eastbrook (J. J. O'Neill) is pursued by Silver Buck (M. Dickinson) in the Sun Alliance Novices' Hurdle at Cheltenham 1978. The race was won by Mr Kildare and Silver Buck finished fourth.

At the line Silver Buck (T. Carmody) romps home clear of Night Nurse (J. J. O'Neill) to win the Edward Hanmer Memorial Chase, November 1979.

Silver Buck jumps the last to win the 1980 Edward Hanmer Memorial Chase.

Mrs Christine Feather and Michael Dickinson with H.M. Queen Elizabeth the Queen Mother after Silver Buck's first King George VI win, Boxing Day 1979.

Tony Dickinson

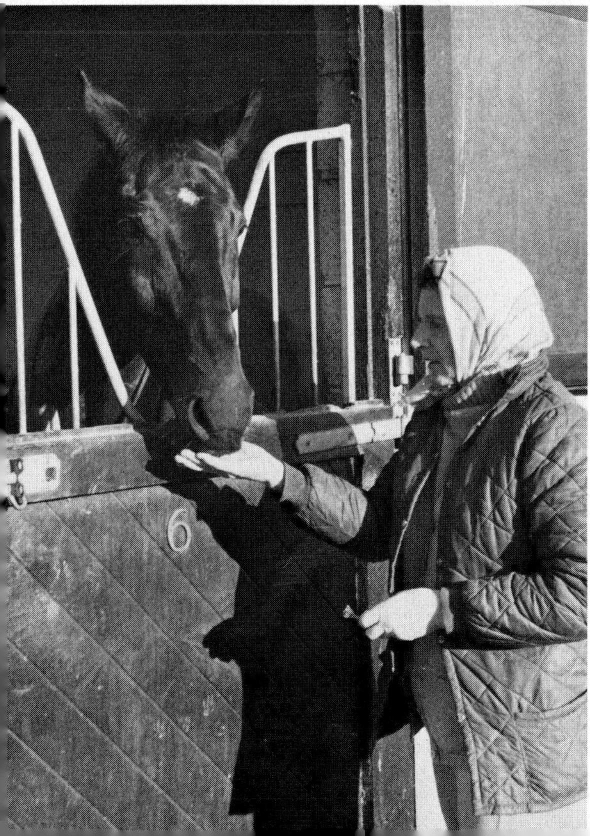

Monica Dickinson with Silver Buck.

Silver Buck (J. Francome up) is led in after winning the Edward Hanmer Memorial Chase 1981.

Silver Buck (R. Earnshaw) clears the last to win the 1982 Cheltenham Gold Cup from stable-companion Bregawn (G. Bradley).

Silver Buck is led in after winning the Cheltenham Gold Cup.

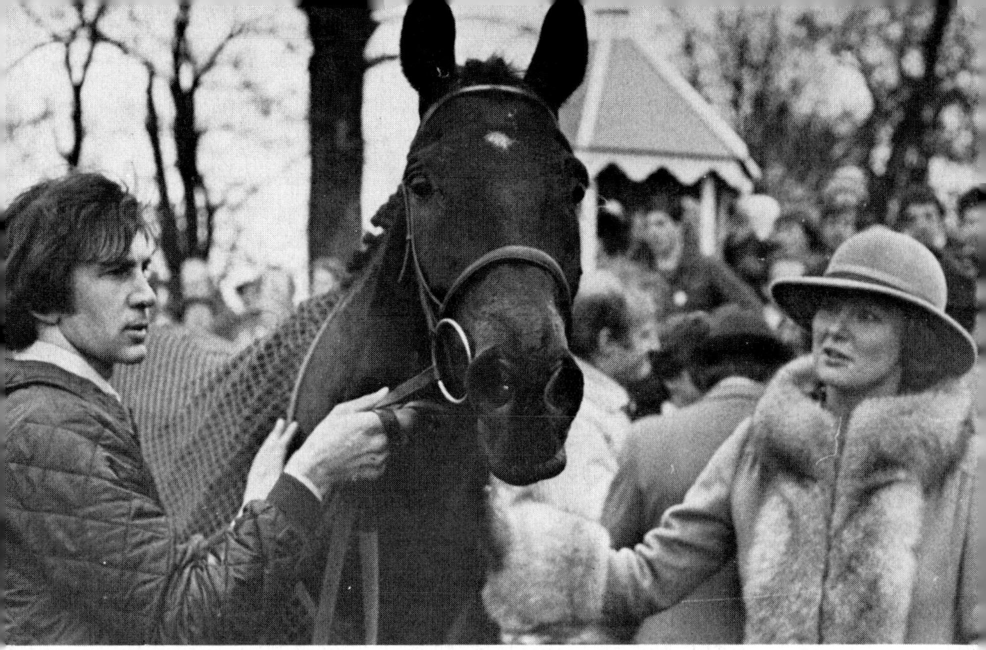

Mrs Christine Feather and Brian Powell (head lad) with Silver Buck.

Over the last in the 1983 Cheltenham Gold Cup in which Silver Buck finished fourth.

Michael Dickinson after his 'Famous Five' triumph in the 1983 Gold Cup.

Silver Buck in the yard at Harewood with young amateur rider Ronnie Beggan.

Seen on the roads near the stables are *left to right:* Planetman (Chris White), Silver Buck (Brian Powell), Righthand Man (Tony Kennedy).

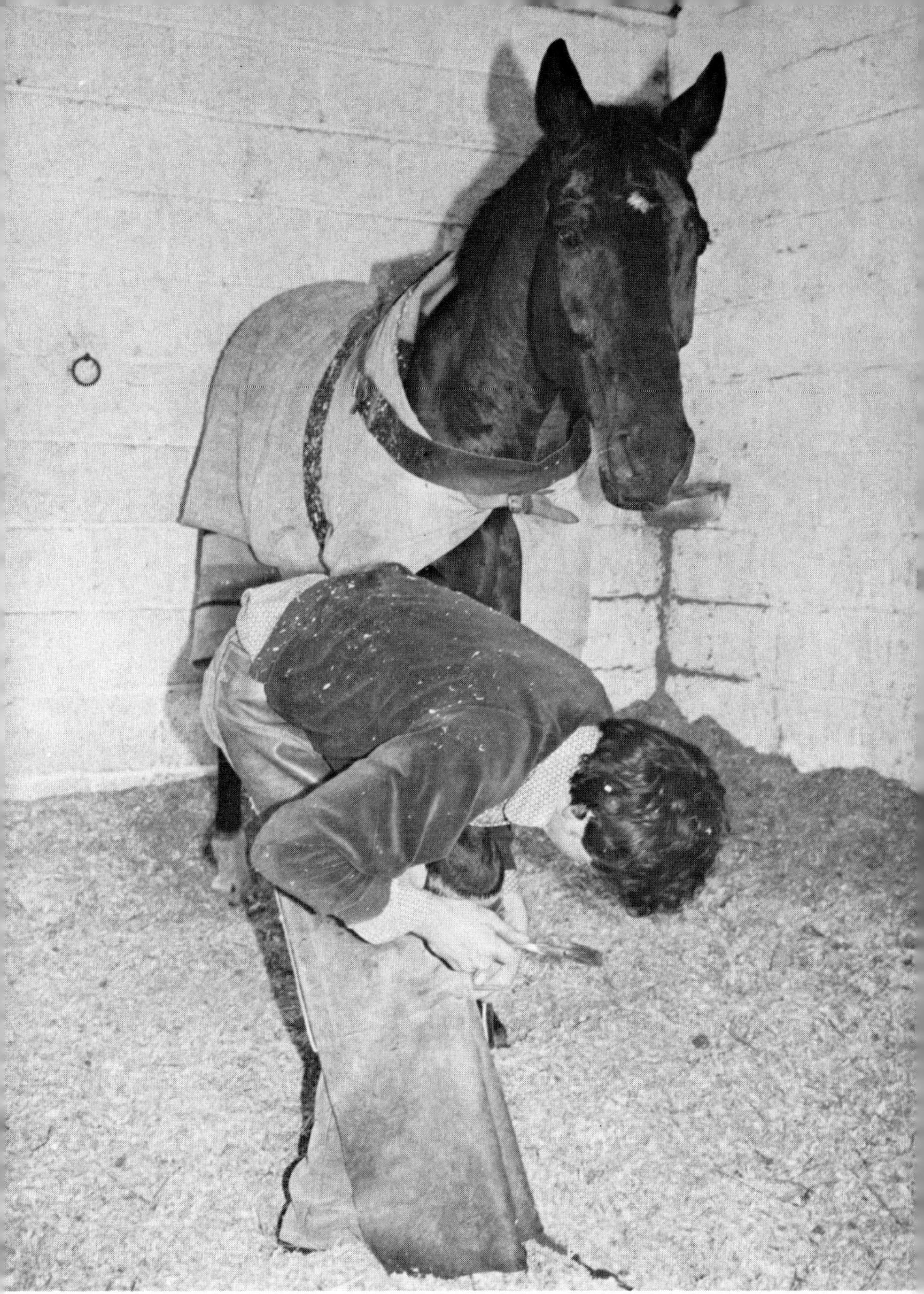

Silver Buck with the blacksmith, Glen Brookes.

Michael Dickinson with head lad Brian Powell and Silver Buck.

the eight meetings to survive.That meant he had the mammoth task of making arrangements for the transporting, saddling and riding of his runners at Kempton, Wetherby, Huntingdon, Market Rasen, Sedgefield and Wolverhampton. Michael elected to supervise his big race candidates at Kempton, where he found the going good to soft, which was unlikely to inconvenience either horse.

The betting was well in line with his evaluation of the King George prospects, Silver Buck starting even money favourite, with Little Owl at 5-2 and Wayward Lad a 7-2 chance (from 4-1). The field was completed by Fifty Dollars More (10-1), Night Nurse (16-1) and the forlorn hope, Foxbury (500-1).

Night Nurse was the early pacemaker but gave way to stablemate Little Owl before the thirteenth fence. When Little Owl had beaten Bregawn at Haydock it might have looked as though he was signalling a return to something like his Gold Cup winning form. But he had been beating a horse with an injured back, and the signals from him on this occasion were only of distress when Silver Buck took him on.

Michael had felt anxious about Silver Buck after the first circuit of the Sunbury course and said to Mrs Feather: 'He's not right.' Robert Earnshaw, too, feared that Silver Buck might not be one hundred per cent, but he was hopeful of winning at the second last, and at that stage Michael and Mrs Feather also had reason to be optimistic.

With Little Owl and Night Nurse beaten off, and Foxbury's partner, Mrs Linda Sheedy, needing binoculars to see what was going on up front, the King George had become a battle between the big three of Silver Buck, Fifty Dollars More and Wayward Lad.

Adding spice to the finish for a Kempton crowd of nearly twenty thousand was the fact that John Francome was on Wayward Lad and not Fifty Dollars More, saddled by his boss, Fred Winter. Fifty Dollars More sports the colours of Sheikh Ali Abu Khamsin, for whom Richard Linley rode regardless of stable.

At the final fence, Robert Earnshaw thought that a good

jump might clinch victory for him. But although Silver Buck took it well he started to weaken and his chance had soon gone. Wayward Lad was sustaining his steady run under John Francome's strong urging, and after getting his nose in front at the last, he kept up a great gallop to beat Fifty Dollars More by two lengths, with Silver Buck a length and a half away in third place.

Michael was disappointed to see Silver Buck 'stop more quickly than he'd ever done before,' and he was sure the performance did not represent his true running. He had plenty to cheer about though with Wayward Lad taking his stable's King George tally to four wins off the reel, the Dickinson domination of the Christmas chasing 'classic' having been initiated by Gay Spartan in 1978 and maintained by Silver Buck's double before the race was abandoned in 1981. Picking up a prize of £24,810 with Wayward Lad turned out to be the icing on a wonderful Christmas cake for the stable.

As the news drifted in of how his representatives at six venues had fared he heard that his stable's amateur Dermot Browne, had ridden a Wolverhampton treble on Brunton Park, Prominent Artist and Slieve Bracken. There was good news for Mrs Feather, too, with her Fearless Imp making a successful seasonal debut under 12st 2lb at Market Rasen, where Chris Pimlott had initiated a Dickinson double with W Six Times.

The jockeys called in to ride for Michael at Huntingdon, Geordie Dun and Richard Rowe, had done their stuff on Marnik and Thornacre. At the stable's local meeting, Wetherby, it was not exactly winners all the way, with Kevin Whyte beaten into second place in three events, but Sooty was saved from a black Christmas by a double on newcomer Delius and staying novice 'chaser, Happy Voyage. With claiming rider Chris Bell winning the last two races at Sedgefield on Londolozi and B Jaski, the Boxing Day bonanza added up to a record-breaking Dickinson dozen, beating by five the previous best one-day tally achieved by that prolific winner-producer from Bishop Auckland, Arthur Stephenson.

Seven runners had finished in the frame to add place prizes to the £3,690 picked up by Silver Buck for his King George third.

When examined on his return to Harewood it was discovered that Silver Buck had a throat infection. Michael then began to have second thoughts about the reason for him 'blowing up' towards the finish of the King George.

'I had thought that it was because he was short of work. But I am sure now, with hindsight, that it was the throat infection.

'We had to send him to Bristol for treatment, but the problem was not thought to be serious, and he was soon back walking up the hills. That was all we could do with him for about three weeks, until he was ready for cantering again. A couple of gallops put him right and he went to Market Rasen, just as he had done the year before.'

The previous year's pattern was also repeated in that Robert Earnshaw was required to ride at Haydock and Kevin Whyte took over on Silver Buck.

Whereas Robert had won the 1982 Timeform Chase on Wayward Lad, this time he had to settle for second best on Branding Iron, who was beaten by the more experienced Fifty Dollars More.

It was a swings and roundabouts situation for him, however, with Righthand Man gamely giving him a Greenall Whitley Chase win to compensate for his near-miss in the race on Bregawn.

Robert has painful memories of his Haydock ride on Happy Voyage, favourite for the three miles Mad Hatter Novices' 'Chase.

'He came down at the first fence and I was knocked unconscious, but fortunately I had no broken bones, although I suffered concussion. I had to miss the ride on Hopeful Saint, a winner in the last race, and I was out of action for a week.'

Robert felt better after receiving the news from Market Rasen that Silver Buck had come through his Cheltenham trial with flying colours. Michael had sent three 'good things' to the Lincolnshire venue and they all obliged, but the bookies ensured that no one would get rich from backing them.

The French importation Sabin du Loir had fifteen lengths to spare in supplying the first leg of the treble at 5-1 on in the Newark Storage Juvenile Hurdle.

Last Deal was an eight lengths scorer in the Victor Lucas Memorial Hurdle at odds of 4-1 on, but when Kevin Whyte, who rode all three, brought Silver Buck home a seven lengths winner of the Budmo Shipping Handicap 'Chase the horse was regarded as such a certainty that no starting price was returned. What a way for Kevin to record his first treble – with a total of thirty lengths to spare! He reported that 'Silver Buck was running away with me'.

Things went according to plan in Bregawn's 'warm up' outing at Hereford, although Graham Bradley had to endure some anxious moments at the start with his mount only getting off at the second attempt. Stable apprentice Graham Burrows was down at the start to lead Bregawn in, but the tapes did not go up at the first try. When the tapes did rise, Bregawn was still being held and he lost about a dozen lengths.

There were no palpitations suffered by punters, however, for Bregawn had looked just as big a certainty as Silver Buck at Market Rasen, and likewise, no starting price was returned. In the circumstances, he would be expected to give the opposition a start and a beating. He made up the lost ground to lead at the seventh fence and then cantered home a distance clear of Pucka Fella and Master Smudge.

Graham Bradley did not blame Bregawn for the tardy start, even though his mount had also lost ground at the off when beaten by Combs Ditch in the Jim Ford Challenge Cup 'Chase at Wincanton just over a week before.

'We were unlucky when he was led in and it was not the horse's fault. He jumped super, and soon went clear when I let out a notch.'

Following a six-timer with Silver Buck, Sabin du Loir, Last Deal, Bregawn, Righthand Man and Hopeful Saint, Michael had saddled twenty-two winners in nine racing days and was left requiring just one more to reach a century for the first time. He remained in the nervous nineties only from Saturday until Tuesday, when Sir Wimpy and Political Pop pulled off a Warwick double.

It was a training century achieved in record time, coming six weeks faster than the previous best ton achieved by Penrith trainer Gordon Richards seven years before.

At this stage of the season the Harewood stable's strike rate was a shade over fifty per cent, with the one hundred and one winners coming from two hundred and one runners.

The bookies paid a tribute to Michael's expertise by making him 5-1 on to win the Cheltenham Gold Cup. He was planning to field a team of five, with Captain John, Ashley House and Wayward Lad lining up alongside Silver Buck and Bregawn.

A leg injury had kept Wayward Lad on the sidelines since his Christmas victory over Fifty Dollars More and Silver Buck and Michael was involved in a race against time to get him fit for Cheltenham.

13 Michael Goes Nap

The tremendous gulf between the mighty and the moderate of the steeplechasing world had been all too evident when a 2½ stones weight differential fell miles short of bridging the gap between Silver Buck and his six Market Rasen rivals.

Consequently, his handicap success under 12st 7lb, even though achieved with such marked superiority, did not mean much when attempting to assess his prospects of winning the Gold Cup for a second time.

With ten days between Robert Earnshaw's fall at Haydock and the opening of the festival fixture, there was no doubt that he would be fully recovered in time to partner Silver Buck. And this year he need have no worries that the ride would not be his, although he was apprehensive about the chances of winning again.

'Silver Buck did not seem to be really at his best and I had to be concerned. He was favourite in the Gold Cup ante-post betting, but Michael told the press in an interview before the Cheltenham meeting that Silver Buck might not be right.

'I think that was the chief reason for Bregawn becoming favourite on the day of the race. And, of course, the pressure on me was eased once everyone knew that Silver Buck was not thought to be as well as he had been when winning the year before.'

The pressure was still very much on Michael Dickinson though, as he prepared five horses for the Tote-sponsored 'chase and several others for major events during Cheltenham's three days. Of the five Cup candidates, Robert Earnshaw thought that Bregawn was the one they all had to beat.

'I did not think that Captain John would be good enough, although he's a very smart steeplechaser. I preferred Wayward Lad to Captain John and Ashley House.

'Wayward Lad stayed three miles over hurdles and I had been confident before the King George that he would get the same distance round Kempton. As to whether he would stay the stiff three-and-a-quarter miles at Cheltenham, I had slight reservations.'

The Gold Cup quintet finished their preparation with a sharpening up spin a couple of days before the race, and then travelled down to Cheltenham on the following day. Michael took the diplomatic view that he ought not to say too much about how the five runners might fare.

'If I voiced a fancy for any particular one, that could upset the other four owners.'

Riding arrangements for Silver Buck (Robert Earnshaw) and Bregawn (Graham Bradley) were as the previous year. Dermot Browne took the mount on Ashley House, with David Goulding and Jonjo O'Neill called in for Captain John and Wayward Lad.

It was still 5-1 on the Dickinson stable winning the Gold Cup, but William Hill's bet 66-1 against the runners filling the first five places. When I mentioned to Michael that Corals offered 33-1 against him not saddling a winner at the festival he inquired: 'How much is £100 on that?'

His tongue in cheek remark began to have the ring of true words spoken in jest when things failed to go right for the Dickinson runners on Cheltenham's day one.

Delius, the first winner of Michael's Boxing Day dozen, was backed from 9-4 to 6-4 in the big meeting's opening Waterford Crystal Supreme Novices' Hurdle. The odds seemed ridiculously short with this relatively inexperienced five-year-old taking on far tougher opposition in a twenty-two-strong field than he had encountered in two wins at Wetherby and a hat-trick success at Stratford.

Dermot Browne's mount was in the fighting line from two hurdles out but was clearly not travelling like a winner. It was Silver Buck's old mate, Tommy Carmody, who came through to lead at the last on Buck House and the combination then held off Golden Friend up the hill to give the Irish a great start to the festival with a one-two. Sunley Builds took third place just ahead of Delius, who could only run on at one pace, but finished lame.

A worse flop was to follow when Branding Iron, on whom Robert Earnshaw sported the black, white and red Silver Buck colours, ran a completely lifeless race in the Arkle Challenge Trophy 'Chase. In marked contrast to his earlier brilliant form over fences, Branding Iron could only plod round the two miles circuit, and the 13-8 favourite never looked like taking a hand in the finish.

At least, there was something for racegoers from the North of England to shout about at Alan Brown brought the Peter Easterby-trained Ryeman home a decisive winner from Boreen Daw and The Tsarevich.

Michael was not represented in either of the next two Waterford Crystal-sponsored events on the card, the Champion Hurdle and Stayers' Hurdle. There was still no joy for followers of favourites as Gaye Brief brought a new dimension to Champion Hurdle form with a superb victory over Boreen Prince and the previous year's winner, For Auction.

The bookies' bags were left bulging like Billy Bunter's tummy after a tuck shop raid when a wide open betting contest for the Stayers' Hurdle resulted in a 50-1 triumph for A Kinsman from the small Cumbria stable of John Brockbank.

The Dickinsons saddled both the favourite, Marnik, and joint second favourite, Rednael, in the Kim Muir Memorial Challenge Cup 'Chase for amateur riders. Rednael was beaten two fences out, and Marnik had been struggling before he came down at the last, where Greasepaint and Colin Magnier were well in command and heading for Ireland's second success of the day.

On an afternoon when only the most clairvoyant of punters could have been getting rich, Michael Dickinson supplied yet another favourite in his Grand Annual Challenge Cup 'Chase representative, Fearless Imp. Getting out was more the order of the day by this time, but market leader Fearless Imp was no good thing at odds of 13-2. Robert Earnshaw's mount was conceding weight all-round and the 23lb advantage enjoyed by Churchfield Boy turned out to be the deciding factor.

A confirmed front-runner, Fearless Imp certainly made more of a mark in the Silver Buck colours than had Branding Iron earlier in the afternoon. But when Mrs Feather might have fancied her horse to lead all the way, along came Joe Byrne with a well-timed challenge on Churchfield Boy to collar the leader and complete a 728-1 treble for Ireland.

The last two of the Emerald Isle's 8-1 threesome had been saddled by Michael Cunningham, handsomely compensating him for the Champion Hurdle defeat of For Auction.

Day two of the meeting dawned with Silver Buck maintaining marginal favouritism over Bregawn in ante-post betting on the following day's Gold Cup.

Michael Dickinson was more preoccupied at that moment with ensuring there were no last minute hitches with regard to the seven horses he saddled at Cheltenham in the afternoon.

He was dually represented in the first two races on the card, and when Sabin Du Loir turned out to be the one to break the Dickinson duck, Michael was as surprised as anyone.

After seeing French importation Sabin du Loir leave his more strongly fancied stablemate, Lettoch (sixth) and the rest of the opposition trailing in the Sun Alliance Novices' Hurdle, a much relieved Michael said that after his first day disappointments he had wondered if there was a bug in the yard.

'When they all got beat I had felt like jumping off the Cheltenham grandstand.'

If Michael needed further express relief from results that had been so indigestable on the opening day, it was supplied with more speed than could have been matched by Alka Seltzer as Badsworth Boy slammed the opposition in the Queen Mother Champion 'Chase.

When Brunton Park ran a great race to beat all except the gambled on Forgive 'N' Forget in the Coral Golden Hurdle Final it was clear that if the Dickinson horses had a bug, there would be a queue of trainers requesting that their horses might be bitten by it.

The success of Badsworth Boy had been slightly soured for Michael when a 'mystery man', who joined the covey of racing correspondents crowding round the trainer for post-race interviews, questioned him about the well-being of Silver Buck. Just before that, the 'mystery man', tall, fair-haired, bespectacled and wearing a bright red pullover under a zip-up jacket, had made people wonder who he was when he stepped forward and shook hands with the Queen Mother immediately after Michael had received her congratulations on Badsworth Boy's success.

When the unknown intruder next invited himself among the press proceedings and fired in a question about the fitness of Silver Buck, Michael could not hide his anger and told him not to ask silly questions. With his face now turning nearly as scarlet as the 'mystery man's' pullover, Michael then told the rest of the gathering: 'I will listen to anyone who has a sensible question, but I'm not answering a pillock like that.' The gate-crasher then wandered off muttering that he thought he had asked a perfectly reasonable question. Security was tightened up in the winner's enclosure after that, but 'mystery man' and red pullover were conspicuous by their absence during the remainder of the meeting.

The Dickinson yard was now really buzzing in anticipation of winning the Gold Cup for the second year. Silver Buck and Bregawn disputed favouritism, but both eased in the market as a gamble developed on Combs Ditch, who was backed from 6-1 to 9-2. Bregawn finally led the betting at 100-30, with Silver Buck drifting to 5-1. Prices of the other Dickinson runners were 6-1 Wayward Lad, 11-1 Captain John and 12-1 Ashley House.

The line-up of eleven in a contest worth £45,260 to the winner included three others from Northern stables, Richdee, Midnight Love and Whiggie Geo, and was completed by the

Fred Winter-trained pair, Fifty Dollars More and Brown Chamberlin.

As Mrs Feather watched the five Dickinson runners having the finishing touches applied to them before they went on parade in the paddock, she thought that the hectic scene would have made a wonderful video film.

'It would have been better than any comedy. There seemed to be about three people with each horse, and they were dashing here and there, passing a bucket about, with Michael, Tony and Monica in the thick of the action. I've never witnessed such organised chaos.'

As far as was humanly possible, however, Michael had every aspect of the situation well under control. He had left nothing to chance, having talked over tactics with his jockeys on a couple of occasions.

It was expected that the 500-1 outsider of the party, Whiggie Geo, would set the early pace. The race went that way, but Nigel Tutty's mount was only allowed to lead for five fences. Graham Bradley then decided to quicken things up and sent Bregawn on at the sixth.

Michael knew that Bregawn would be beaten for speed if they didn't go a good gallop. He just hoped that Graham would judge it right and not go too fast.

Robert Earnshaw was in no hurry to send Silver Buck after the leader, who had gone well clear.

'Bregawn was setting a strong gallop and I knew that he would keep going. At the top of the hill, where I wanted to be handy, we were in contention, but after that, Silver Buck gradually weakened.'

Captain John and Wayward Lad now loomed up as the dangers to Bregawn, whose lead had been drastically reduced at the third last.

A blunder at this fence cost Captain John valuable ground but David Goulding got him back on an even keel to maintain his challenge.

Wayward Lad was also keeping up the pressure on Bregawn but Jonjo O'Neill felt his mount 'blow up' as that spell on the sidelines due to injury took its toll.

When Bregawn cleared the final fence to a roar befitting a big race favourite performing before a crowd of 36,577, there was no Silver Buck standing between him and the Gold Cup glory on this occasion.

As Graham Bradley rode Bregawn out to win decisively, if at full stretch, by five lengths from Captain John, with Wayward Lad a further one-and-a-half lengths away, the remarkable Gold Cup feat of Michael Dickinson was still unfolding.

A distance behind in fourth place came Silver Buck, followed another twenty-five lengths away by Ashley House, and the five-horse domination of the great 'chase was complete.

Michael, who, like the year before, had watched the race on TV, said: 'I didn't shout for any one of the horses, just for the boys. As the horses came over the last, I wasn't just proud of them, but of those who had looked after them.

'I worried so much while preparing the five horses that I lost a stone in weight. You need luck to get one horse fit for Cheltenham.

'I had thought that Whiggie Geo would stay in the lead longer than he did, but Brad's judgment was spot on. If Bregawn had not gone fast enough he could have been beaten for speed. Brad did it just right.'

The Cheltenham executive was not slow to allow special dispensation for the 'fantastic five' to be allowed into the unsaddling enclosure, the racecourse chairman, Captain Miles Gosling, commenting: 'This feat will never be seen again and we gave permission for the fifth horse to go into the enclosure along with the first four.'

Michael Dickinson was particularly delighted that in the midst of all the hand-shaking and back-slapping he received the warmest congratulations from Silver Buck's ever-sporting owner Mrs Feather.

'She would have been entitled to feel cross that Silver Buck had finished a well-beaten fourth. After all, I had failed to deliver him at the post fit enough to do any better.

'Chris was a wonderful sport and just happy that I had

won the Gold Cup again. It made no difference which horse was the winner.

'She flung her arms round me and gave me two big kisses, and I thought she was tremendous. You couldn't imagine Daniel Wildenstein doing that to Henry Cecil after one of his horses had run badly, could you?'

14 Back on the Winning Trail

Silver Buck was already back on the winning trail when the announcement was made in late November of the 1983-84 season that Michael Dickinson would be quitting the jumping game to become private trainer to millionaire pools boss, Robert Sangster.

The move to stables formerly belonging to Arthur Budgett, at Whatcombe, where the Derby winners Blakeney (1969) and Morston (1973) had been trained, was to be two years hence. Michael's switch came as no real surprise, the newspapers having carried reports for some time that he was seeking a larger establishment where he would have three hundred acres at his disposal, compared with the one hundred acres – plus another hundred acres that was rented – at Poplar House, Harewood. This conjecture mainly centred on the possibility of Michael finding such a place in Yorkshire, although he seemed to have ruled out that hope when he said: 'It could take years'.

The tie-up with Robert Sangster had not been anticipated by the media, but Michael had kept his owners well-informed and received their blessing before the news hit the headlines of the racing pages. When Michael popped in to see Mrs Feather, who lives close to Harewood, and told her he was taking the plunge, her only thought at first was 'what will happen to dear old Bucket?'

She had talked to Michael about his permutation of possible moves for a long time before, and foresaw the decision that he was destined to take.

'The offer was so colossal he could hardly be expected to refuse it. Obviously, I will be sorry to see him go, but I am just proud that Silver Buck was in the yard when Michael took over and that my horse has been part of the success story. I have always had a great relationship with him – probably because I have done what I was told!'

Michael stressed that his parents had made his decision so much easier by their willingness to come out of retirement and take over the jumpers. Mrs Feather quickly gave the new arrangements a vote of confidence by stating: 'My horses will certainly be staying with Tony and Monica.'

Winners are food and drink to Michael, a man of unquenchable ambitions, and he was soon emphasising: 'There will be no winding down of the operation during the two seasons I have left at Harewood.'

At the same time, those two years would also be used to plan his future with the maximum of care, and it was true to the type of dedication that had taken him so far up the training tree at the age of thirty-three, that he envisaged himself walking most of the flat courses to find out at first hand exactly what was required to win on each one.

He anticipated the Harewood horse-power being cut back to about forty when his parents took over the reins. How did Tony Dickinson, at the age of sixty-eight, view the prospect of making a training come-back?

'My experience will obviously stand me in good stead, and, of course, Monica is very active and she will continue to play an important role in the running of the stable. But I am not getting any younger and will need a good man to help me.

'After Michael's accident at Cartmel which ended his riding career, I was able to give him the right kind of start as a trainer.

'I handed over forty good owners and their horses after training ninety-four winners in my last season. We were not the top for prize money that season – Peter Easterby beat us – but we had more winners than anyone else.

'We came up the hard way from those early days at Gisburn, and since then our determination to look after the owners' interests has consistently paid dividends. I don't believe in hanging on to bad horses, and wasting owners' time and money. If a horse is not good enough I always tell the owner.

'I am very pleased that Michael has got such a wonderful opportunity to train on the flat. It is a chance that he could not possibly miss and I am sure he will be successful. Michael's shrewd placing of our horses has been the key to much of our success. I only hope I can find an assistant with half of his talent for choosing the right races.'

Before the time came for Michael to gallop away from the Gold Cup trail in a direction surely signposted to eventual Epsom Derby success, he hoped to take a couple of cracks at winning the Aintree Grand National.

'That is the main big target left for me over jumps, but I have only two more opportunities to achieve it, and there are great trainers who have never won a National in a lifetime.

'I love the jumping game, but I decided that if I was ever to switch to the flat the best time would be while I was still young, and I couldn't see myself training jumpers for another twenty years. I spent the summer pondering over the decision and it was not until the end of September that I decided the time was ripe.'

While a Grand National triumph would be a wonderful way to set the seal on Michael's jumping career, I am sure he would be equally happy to bow out with another King George or Gold Cup victory by Silver Buck. Incidentally, there was no truth in the rumour that Michael decided to pack up as a jumping trainer because of Silver Buck's impending retirement!

At the start of the season Michael had reported: 'Silver Buck certainly doesn't look his age, but injury is the main threat to a horse's career, rather than age. Red Rum would probably have gone on for another couple of seasons but for injury. And it was a similar story with Arkle. It is usually a sudden injury that gets them.'

Silver Buck's seasonal debut was delayed when he needed time to recover from a bump on the knee, and it was in mid-November that he returned to action, at Folkestone. Mrs

Feather decided that Folkestone was too far for her to travel just to see Bucket going through the formality of beating three opponents in the Whitelaw Gold Cup 'Chase.

'It made more sense for my son, William, to represent me there. He is assistant trainer to John Winter, at Newmarket, so he is a lot nearer to Folkestone than I am.'

After seeing Silver Buck, who started at 7-1 on, beat the second favourite, Iden Green (8-1), by three lengths, William reported to his mother that the Folkestone going had been firmer than Bucket appreciated and that the horse looked a little 'tucked up' before the race, possibly because he was feeling the very cold wind whistling around the south-eastern track.

Robert Earnshaw said that he was well satisfied with Silver Buck's running, not having expected his old pal to do more than was necessary in a four-horse affair.

Michael decided to reserve judgment on the merit of the performance, but wondered if Silver Buck had been up to his old tricks, 'thinking that he had done enough because he was in front'. Michael added: 'He always wins first time out, but is rarely impressive. And he may not have been all that fit, although the lad who led him up said he didn't blow a lot.

'On the plus side, he has had an outing, and came through the race well. I will gallop him at the weekend and then we might be a little wiser.'

The critics, searching for signs of Silver Buck cracking up now that he was in the veteran stage, thought that the brown gelding looked a shadow of his former self despite his clear superiority over Iden Green. William Hill's representative, Mike Cowtan, was quoted in the *Sporting Life* as saying that Silver Buck was 'unimpressive', and that, 'sadly, he will never win another Gold Cup'.

In the light of Cowtan's comment, Hill's offer of 9-1 in ante-post betting on the Tote-sponsored 'chase was not over-generous, remembering that Silver Buck had started at only a point less when he struck 'Gold' in 1982.

A few opinions might well have been revised when Iden Green went on to storm home a seven lengths winner from

Mr Marlsbridge in Ascot's two miles Charles Davis Handicap 'Chase. On the morning of that particular contest – for which Iden Green started at 5-1 – the Folkestone runner-up was priced at 10-1 in Ladbrokes shops.

Punters wise enough not to knock the Folkestone form certainly had the opportunity to snap up a rare bargain that day, although some icing was taken from the cake by the deduction of 30p in the pound from winnings because of the withdrawal of Pretty Hopeful.

Reflecting on Iden Green's running at Folkestone, trainer Gardie Grissel said: 'The press men are usually good race readers, but they tended to regard my horse's running against Silver Buck as a fluke. In view of the Ascot outcome, it now looks as though they were wrong. I am sure that Silver Buck could have pulled out some more, but the race was run in very good time.'

Iden Green proceeded to give Silver Buck another boost by winning a Newbury 'match' against Bashful Lad in the Jacky Upton 'Chase. This kind of form might be far removed from top-class but Silver Buck's debut run had, at least, been made to look respectable.

The Folkestone run had been intended to bring Silver Buck to concert pitch before taking the stage at Haydock for his attempt to win the Edward Hanmer for the fifth time off the reel.

Michael was pleased by Silver Buck's subsequent homework, but with ground conditions remaining very firm in an exceptionally dry November, he was reluctant to risk the veteran running again before there was some rain. He told Mrs Feather of his fears, and it was decided that Wayward Lad, who had started the season with an impressive win on fast ground at Wetherby, should be the stable's Edward Hanmer representative.

With the majority of other trainers equally worried by the virtually dust-dry conditions, withdrawals were wholesale for most meetings at the overnight declaration stage. Haydock's opening card cut up to leave a total of only twenty-four runners, with the featured Edward Hanmer retaining only three. The programme looked farcical, and that all too frequent visitor to winter jumping venues, Jack Frost, must have felt the same way, a swipe from his icy fingers putting the two-day fixture completely out in the cold.

That left Michael with the task of re-routing Wayward Lad, and he chose the Peterborough 'Chase at Huntingdon on the following Tuesday. In the meantime, milder weather returned, and there was rain about, so Silver Buck was despatched along with Mrs Feather's smart two-miler, Fearless Imp, to fulfil a Saturday engagement at Market Rasen. Mrs Feather was well pleased with arrangements that enabled her to 'kill two birds with one stone', although Michael joked that it would mean she only had one day out instead of two. It was a day of double delight for her, however, when Fearless Imp, partnered by Dermot Browne, made a successful seasonal debut over the minimum distance in the Chase Handicap 'Chase and Silver Buck won a weight-conceding match against Medway Gauntlet in the three miles Limes Handicap 'Chase.

Silver Buck's three quarters of a length victory – achieved with plenty to spare – satisfied all concerned, and gave immense pleasure to Kevin Whyte, who was making a habit of coming in for the ride whenever Bucket went to Market Rasen.

Robert Earnshaw had been required for Marnik in the Hennessy at Newbury, enabling Sootie to step in as super sub. While Silver Buck did nothing spectacular, he left Kevin enthusing: 'That old sparkle is still there and I think he's as good as ever. With not having any horses around him, he was playing about and taking his time at the fences. I couldn't trust him at a fence, but he's very cute and there was no danger of him falling. When Medway Gauntlet came to him at the last, I just gave him a bit of a kick and he quickened up so well that it seemed like he only had 10st and not 12st 7lb on his back.

'He has gone lazier than ever, but he's just the same at home nowadays. At one time, there were only two people who could ride him, but anyone would be able to get on him now.'

Understandably itching for an opportunity to team up with Bucket in the big time, Kevin sighed: 'I would love to ride him in a "proper" race.' And that after maintaining an unbeaten record on Silver Buck in three rides – all at Market Rasen, when shouldering 12st 7lb in handicaps. Kevin rates his first ride on Silver Buck, when his mount gave 2½ stones to Moor Close, the best of the three.

'There were nine runners in the field and Silver Buck had something to take him on. Moor Close was receiving a lot of weight, but although he put in a challenge over the last three fences, Bucket was always holding him without being extended. After that, I could not see how he was going to be beaten at Cheltenham.

'It was wonderful to see him win the Gold Cup, so that he got the recognition he deserved. He is a great horse, a tremendous character.'

Mrs Feather was quick to praise both winning jockeys – and her trainer – after their combined efforts had provided her first double.

'I had never had two runners on the same card before and it was tremendously exciting to see them both win. Dermot Browne gave Fearless Imp a superb ride – no wonder he's the top amateur!

'And while it was a shame that Robert had to miss the ride on Silver Buck because of his Newbury commitment, it was nice to see Kevin Whyte getting another chance to win on him after all the time and effort he has devoted to Bucket at home.

'I shall be writing to Michael Dickinson to congratulate him and his staff on the way those two horses were turned out at Market Rasen. Each one looked a picture as he was brought into the parade ring.'

Michael thought that Silver Buck's second outing indicated that he had improved since the Folkestone win.

'He was fitter at Market Rasen and I will give him another race at Nottingham. Then he should be fitter still, and just right for the King George three weeks later.'

Silver Buck's successes at Folkestone and Market Rasen

took his total earnings – including place prizes – to £180,750.50.

Wayward Lad – hot in pursuit of Silver Buck's handsome prize money haul – compensated his connections for the loss of the Haydock opportunity by beating Fifty Dollars More in Huntingdon's Peterborough 'Chase, but it was only by a short head that Robert Earnshaw's mount confirmed his previous season's King George superiority over the Fred Winter-trained horse, ridden by Richard Linley.

With Wayward Lad, Fifty Dollars More and Silver Buck now primed for another epic clash at Kempton, the jump fans would be living in dread of a white Christmas as they dreamed of the trio once again coming to the final fence in line for another last ditch, titanic tussle.

Plans for Silver Buck were destined to be revised, however, during the four weeks' build-up to the Boxing Day contest. They say that only a fool never changes his mind, and Michael was certainly no mug when it came to selecting the right race for any horse. Nevertheless, you can't win them all and in deciding to give Nottingham a miss and saddle Silver Buck at Chepstow a couple of days earlier, Michael was passing up what turned out to be a very easy opportunity. Not that Chepstow's Rehearsal Chase – the more valuable race of the two – looked all that hard to win and Silver Buck started 7-4 on. But in a four-horse affair, he met more than his match in the 6-4 second favourite, Observe.

Sointulla Boy was soon tailed off and with Another Breeze struggling after leading until the sixth, the issue then clearly rested between Silver Buck and Observe. When John Francome started putting Observe under pressure before the turn for home it seemed as though Silver Buck, who was holding a slight advantage, might have cracked his labouring rival. The harder Francome worked, however, the more Observe responded and after his mount had jumped just that little bit better than Silver Buck at the second last, it was Robert Earnshaw's turn to get worried and resort to the whip. Silver Buck could find no more as Observe galloped on gamely to triumph by two-and-a-half lengths after the prolonged battle. Francome's determination, although rewarded with victory, cost him a £75 fine when the Chepstow stewards found him guilty of using the whip with excessive force. Ironically, the Newbury stewards had slapped a similar fine on him in Observe's seasonal debut race because he failed to ride out the horse for second place.

If the Chepstow result was disappointing for Michael Dickinson it was no consolation for him when the Nottingham event that Silver Buck missed, the Last Chance Chase, cut up into a match between Scot Lane and Antic. This turned out to be a disastrous race for Craig Smith, who broke his right leg when odds-on Scot Lane slipped almost to his knees on greasy ground between the fifth and sixth fences on the bottom bend and gave the jockey no chance of staying in the saddle. Scot Lane, ridden by Peter Scudamore, was in opposition when Silver Buck made his next racecourse appearance.

Michael Dickinson had decided during the fortnight before the King George that it made more sense to reserve Silver Buck – now dropped in the weights – for a valuable handicap assignment rather than take on the cracks at levels. This arrangement suited Mrs Feather, because it left the way clear for Robert Earnshaw to partner Wayward Lad.

'I did not want Robert to be in the position of having to ride one or the other. It was obviously in his best interests to maintain his association with the younger horse, who should still be competing in the top class when Silver Buck has retired.'

Robert gave Wayward Lad a really great ride in extending the Dickinsons' King George monopoly to five wins in a row, the combination breaking the Kempton course record by more than eight seconds in overcoming Brown Chamberlin and The Mighty Mac.

A week later – and a day after Silver Buck's twelfth birthday – Robert was teaming up with his old favourite again at Cheltenham.

Looking a handicap snip in a Courage Cup Qualifier, Silver Buck attracted confident support to start a 5-2 on chance.

His backers turned out to be good judges. But his owner was an ever better judge! She was sunning herself in Portugal as the gale-lashed Cheltenham crowd bravely mustered a cheer to salute Silver Buck's mastery of Scot Lane and four other opponents.

Robert Earnshaw had got off the thirteen mark for the season in the previous race when initiating a Dickinson double on Santella King. His reward when he returned to Harewood was a roasting from Michael for 'coming too soon' on Silver Buck. Such criticism is all in the day's work and fully justified in the complete professional's pursuit of perfection.

15 Mrs Feather's Friend

Silver Buck entered Mrs Christine Feather's life shortly after the exit of her first husband. Some married people might joke that they wouldn't mind a similar swap. At the time, however, for Christine, then Mrs Haggas, the situation was nothing less than serious as she recalls in the following pages.

My husband had left me and I was at the bottom of the pile. If anything, it was my interest in racing, and in particular the acquisition of Silver Buck, that turned out to be my saviour. We had been involved with flat racing for some time before deciding not to be left out of the jumping game. My father-in-law had two very good horses, The Chisler and Headsprite, and they were trained by Tony Dickinson, who was then based at Gisburn. Grannie and Grandpa Haggas bought me my first race horse, Tempting Times, as a Christmas present. He did win once with Michael in the saddle.

It was Tony and his wife Monica who had a lot to do with lifting me out of the doldrums following the break up of my marriage. Mr first husband, Brian, had been gone over a year when they rang and asked me to come over to the stables the following day to take a look at a couple of horses. One of them was Silver Buck and the other Cavity Hunter. They did this because they knew that Tempting Times, who had been injured, would have to be put down.

I fell, hook, line and sinker for Cavity Hunter. I didn't really look at Silver Buck at all. He was extremely nervous, and seemed very moody and spooky. When you went into his box he would shunt right up into the corner.

I said, 'Right, Tony, I'll have Cavity Hunter.' Tony was agreeable, and I thought, great! He told me to come back on Sunday morning and bring my cheque book.

Anyway, a couple of days later, I had a phone call from him. 'I've got something terrible to tell you,' he said.

Then he explained: 'Frank Tyldesley, who is my biggest owner, has been for lunch. He has seen Cavity Hunter and he's very keen to buy him.'

Then Tony appealed: 'He's getting on Chris. Would you be a real lady and have Silver Buck instead?'

'Tony,' I said, 'I'm so desperate for a horse I'll have anything.' And that is how I became the owner of Silver Buck.

I went to the stables on the Sunday morning to complete the deal, and Robin Feather, who was to become my second husband, came along with me.

'I was buying Silver Buck from the Skipton solicitor, Jack Mewies. I didn't think to ask him why he was selling the horse. He just said: 'The best of luck with him.' Silver Buck had won over hurdles both for Mr Mewies and Monica Dickinson, whose colours he carried when he first came over from Ireland.

It was anybody's guess as to whether he would eventually make a steeplechaser. But his first race for me was over hurdles at the Cheltenham festival meeting in 1978. He was fourth in the Sun Alliance Novices' Hurdle, with Michael Dickinson riding him. Tommy Carmody, who didn't know then that he would be coming into the Dickinsons' yard, was on the winner Mr Kildare. Tommy won the following race, too, on Hilly Way.

Silver Buck's next outing was at Liverpool, where he finished a bit lame. I don't think he should have run either at Cheltenham or Liverpool. The Dickinsons probably ran him in those races at the big meetings just to please me. I doubt whether he was really right.

He was retired for the season and spent a lot of his time during that summer in a field at Gisburn along with Gay Spartan. They were virtually inseparable.

I have every reason to remember the day – May 27, 1978

— that Michael Dickinson had the terrible fall from Buck Me Off at Cartmel which was to end his riding career. It was the twenty-first birthday of my eldest son, James.

Michael was a very, very poorly man for a long time. After all he had gone through, I was very relieved when he decided he would have to give up riding.

All the owners connected with the stables were consulted to see whether it would be best to have a retained jockey or not. The consensus of opinion was that Tommy Carmody was the man for the job.

Tommy was retained and became stable jockey from the start of the 1978-79 season. He soon struck up a successful steeplechasing partnership with Silver Buck. They won four in a row including a very fine performance by Silver Buck when he beat Alverton at Wetherby.

Then the snow came in December and he had a little rest. The weather was appalling and the race intended as Silver Buck's major target, the Embassy Premier 'Chase Final, was put back from January to March.

Silver Buck and Gay Spartan were entered for about eight races within the space of five days in the hope that they might get a run somewhere or other. Fortunately, the weather broke just before the last week in February and Gay Spartan was able to go for Wincanton's Jim Ford Challenge Cup, while Silver Buck went to Windsor for the Fairlawne 'Chase.

Silver Buck had the bad luck to be brought down in a race which had looked a formality for him to win. But if that was disappointing, I experienced one of the most exciting days of my life when Silver Buck ran in the rearranged Embassy Premier Final, at Haydock Park.

I was just hopeful that Silver Buck would win. My attitude is that if both the jockey and the horse get round, and thoroughly enjoy themselves, then I'm happy. If they win it's a bonus. I can't bear horses to fall. That really upsets me.

The Dickinsons are fairly secretive. You can ask them a thousand and one questions and they'll tell you what they think you ought to know. Not that I read anything into it. But I wouldn't have pretended to know what the instructions were to Tommy Carmody before he rode Silver Buck in the Haydock race. That matter had obviously been dealt with during the week before. Nothing was mentioned in the paddock.

What a tremendously thrilling event the Embassy Final turned out to be. Going round the bend into the back straight, Silver Buck and Night Nurse were racing together. They stayed like that, stride for stride, all the way down the far side. They were miles in front of the others, and literally neck and neck. After jumping the last, Bucket lost his concentration. There's a fence where they have to come slightly to the left on the run to the winning post. We were screaming and yelling, 'Come on Bucket', and giving him all the encouragement we could.

Galloping past this fence he was having a good look at it, as if to say: 'Why the hell can't I jump it?' He had to have a couple of cracks from Tommy to straighten him out, but he went on to beat Night Nurse by two-and-a-half lengths.

Then, of course, we realised that we possessed a top-class 'chaser. It was tremendously exciting. I had won races before, but this was the first really big one.

Silver Buck was in the *Sporting Life* headlines the following day. And my friend, Lord Oaksey, was reporting in the *Telegraph* that Night Nurse would be all the better for the race. John loved Night Nurse and I pulled his leg about it.

People sent flowers and there were telegrams. It was a peculiar feeling that my little boy had done it. Not forgetting, of course, the credit due to the trainer and jockey.

With Silver Buck doing his stuff so magnificently at Haydock everybody had high hopes of him winning the Sun Alliance 'Chase at Cheltenham's big meeting. However, the ground was very heavy for the festival and Silver Buck didn't like it. The conditions suited Master Smudge, who won from Sweet September, with Silver Buck in third place.

I had gone to see Bucket in his box before the race. Michael, Tony and Monica were dashing around as busy as bees. To my astonishment – and amusement – there was Silver Buck standing with one corner of a tea towel stuck up his nose. He hardly looked wildly attractive, and the towel was soon whipped away when they saw me. It gave me a great laugh. The tea towel was being used because Silver Buck had a bit of a dirty nose. And when he returned home he was found to have a temperature. So he wouldn't have been right for the Sun Alliance.

After his summer's rest, I was eagerly looking forward to seeing him in action again by the time he went to Wincanton for the Terry Biddlecombe 'Chase at the beginning of November. He won comfortably there and followed up at Hereford before coming out on top in another memorable clash with Night Nurse in the Edward Hanmer Memorial at Haydock.

I think they took him to Market Rasen for a charge round over hurdles before he ran in the King George on Boxing Day. Michael and Tony didn't go to Kempton. Monica came with us, and Michael's cousin, Robert Dickinson, did the saddling with Tommy Stack assisting him. The whole Boxing Day trip for the King George is pandemonium. You have to be up at 6 o'clock – and that's not easy at the best of times, let alone after Christmas Day. It was all worth while when Silver Buck beat Jack of Trumps, and that set us up for the long journey home. We were absolutely shattered when we arrived back at the stables. By then Tony, Michael and the rest of the team had returned from other meetings. It has become a Boxing Day ritual for us to hold a get-together and tell of our triumphs or relate hard luck stories.

Silver Buck's winning run continued at Newbury where the weather was foul and ground conditions bad, but he put up a good performance to beat Royal Mail in the Compton 'Chase.

Then he went to Hereford and how Tommy Carmody didn't come off him when he made a terrible mistake I don't know. God must have been watching him. Silver Buck produced his only good jump of the race at the final fence, and that was where Portway Nick blundered his chance away. But for that, Portway Nick might have caused a real upset, because Silver Buck was 6-1 on. It was the worst jumping display I had seen from him, and ill-timed too with the Gold Cup coming up. Not that it made any difference in the end because heavy going at Cheltenham ruled him out of the race. I was bitterly disappointed, but could console myself by looking back on a season during which he was unbeaten and had won the King George.

If Silver Buck had won the Gold Cup the following year, I would not have been at Cheltenham to see it. The weather was turning foul again as the festival approached so we packed our bags and went on holiday to Barbados. We heard the news via a betting shop in Barbados that Silver Buck had finished third to Little Owl and Night Nurse.

The Dickinson horses didn't seem to be running up to their true form just then, although Political Pop was a winner at Cheltenham. I was beginning to think that this course was not Silver Buck's scene, although his record there was not bad – fourth over hurdles and twice third in chases, all big events at the festival. It was just that the sparkle he showed at Kempton had yet to be produced at Cheltenham.

The horse had done us proud during the season with his five wins including a memorable victory over Anaglog's Daughter to complete a double in the King George. Anaglog's Daughter had set off like a lunatic in her usual way – what a brave animal, and how she could gallop and keep it up! Night Nurse was having another set-to with Silver Buck until he made a mess of the last fence and put Alan Brown on the floor. That was after Brown had managed to stay on board when Night Nurse clouted the seventeenth. It was ironic that they should part company after absolutely pinging the second last. The Queen Mother was marvellous when she made the King George presentation. What with meeting Royalty after the race, and doing the 'bucket job' before it while Silver Buck was being saddled, there was never a dull moment at Kempton.

At the start of the 1981-82 season, I was nagging Michael to run Silver Buck in a two-and-a-half miles 'chase at Cheltenham, like the Mackeson Gold Cup. But he would hear none of it, saying that the opposition would run him off his feet over the shorter distance and that he would have far too much weight. By this time I had acquired a few other horses. I haven't been lucky with hurdlers, and when I bought Hugo di Tours he turned out to be no exception to my misfortunes. He had been trained on the flat by Luca Cumani, at Newmarket, and was a lovely horse. Hugo di Tours ran only once for me in a novices' hurdle, at Nottingham. He had never hurdled before, but he started hot favourite. Two horses fell in front of him and he over-reached. We could never get the injured leg right again. I bought Fearless Imp to go 'chasing after he had won hurdles for John Truman, who bred him.

I had a couple of hectic but enjoyable days watching Silver Buck and Fearless Imp in action during October of the 1981-82 season. We had to travel down to Wincanton for Silver Buck's first outing of the season, and then whizz back for Fearless Imp's race at Wetherby the following day. Silver Buck took the Terry Biddlecombe 'Chase easily enough and Fearless Imp made it a double by winning his first attempt over fences. There were twenty runners in Fearless Imp's race and it was thrilling to see him making all the running and never looking likely to be caught. At the finish he had eight lengths to spare over Onapromise.

Things, however, rarely run smoothly for very long in racing and Silver Buck's next outing at Chepstow turned out to be a disaster. I didn't like the way he carried on while he was being saddled. He looked all right, but he was fidgeting all the time. During the race he looked so tired, and ran with no life at all. He usually took quite a hold to begin with, but there was nothing like that. The jump before he fell, he just scrambled over and by that time Straight Jocelyn was miles in front. We didn't actually see him fall, it's difficult to see that particular fence from the stands at Chepstow. Silver Buck was so tired that when he fell he didn't move away, but just waited for Robert, who was a little concussed, to remount him, but they walked back together. Robert said he daren't get back on him.

When Michael decided to send Silver Buck to Haydock for the Edward Hanmer Memorial less than three weeks later, he felt that he was putting his head on the block. He did not think that the horse was one hundred per cent fit and would have been happy to see him finish third or fourth, so long as he ran well.

Much to our surprise, and relief, Bucket was absolutely brilliant. John Francome, having his first ride for the Dickinson stable, told us after the race that he was really pulling his arms out from the second last. Royal Bond was close up when he came down at the last fence, but John said that Silver Buck would have beaten him.

Our hopes were now high that Bucket could become the first horse to complete a King George hat-trick. He was in great heart until Christmas Eve and then suddenly we had an extremely lame horse on our hands. He had obviously trodden on something in his box. It could have been a nail, and maybe he had been injured by his shoe coming off. I have never had a proper story about it. He really was very, very lame, but the injury did not cost him his chance of another win in the King George. Both days of the Kempton meeting were abandoned because of frost, so that left us with all to play for in the Cheltenham Gold Cup, provided we could get him fit again.

The Dickinsons and their staff worked night and day to put him right, bathed his injured leg, and poulticed it. They did everything they possibly could. George Foster, one of their lads, is very good with sick horses. You could call him a vet without any qualifications. He attended to Silver Buck all hours of the day and night. The treatment was completely successful and all the credit goes to that lad, George Foster.

After Silver Buck had been confined to his box for a month, Kevin Whyte had the job of walking the horse – and they walked for miles! The dedication of both George and Kevin enabled Bucket to run at Market Rasen with just twelve days to go before the Gold Cup. We were absolutely over the moon when he carried 12st 7lb to victory against eight opponents receiving 2st and upwards from him. After three months off the racecourse it was a marvellous come-back performance. It was further proof that Silver Buck could carry a big weight in a handicap – and win!

The injury to Silver Buck may have been a blessing in disguise. He had been kept off the course during the middle of winter, and with the benefit of the Market Rasen run, I doubt if he had ever been better when Cheltenham came around. He looked in tremendous shape and ran the race of his life. The speed that Silver Buck showed as he came down the hill and round the bend into the straight was unbelievable. Bregawn was the only one able to keep in touch with him, but he was always fighting a losing battle, and Graham Bradley knew it. Silver Buck made a few doubters eat their words that day. Not only did he stay the distance, but he won on ground softer than he was supposed to like.

After all the excitement in the winner's enclosure, we went to have drinks with the Queen Mother, who is always so charming. The Prince of Wales was there and Michael was presented to him.

The Prince said: 'How clever to have the first two, but don't you think you're pushing your luck a bit by running two and having them both there at the finish?'

Michael replied: 'Oh, it's nothing to do with me sir. It's all down to Capt. Gosling's drains.'

This brought the house down because they had spent so much money at Cheltenham on drainage work, and Capt. Gosling was the racecourse chairman.

When the Queen Mother presented the trophy to Michael she said: 'You can't have any ambition left now.'

Michael, with real aplomb, replied: 'I have ma'am. When you win the Gold Cup, I would like to make the presentation to you!'

Winning the Gold Cup was magic, a really happy occasion. If you are lucky enough to have a horse like Silver Buck it is amazing the doors that open to you. There was another cause for celebration when Silver Buck became champion jumper, at the same time that Shergar was champion on the flat. It was a most memorable evening when the awards were presented at the Racehorse of the Year dinner at York. I sat next to Shergar's owner, the Aga Khan, and received the award from Pat Muldoon, whose super hurdler, Sea Pigeon, was champion jumper the year before.

Then we decided we would have our own party, 'Silver Buck at home.' About 300 people came – everybody from the farrier and stable lads, to jockeys, owners, trainers and friends. The lads were a bit cross with me because I asked them to wear a badge with their name on it. They didn't want to do it, but I said, 'Now look, I've talked to Michael about it and he agrees with me. There are a lot of people coming who are very interested in all of you. Wouldn't it be nice if someone came up to you and said . . . "I know you. Didn't you ride such and such a thing?" ' Anyway, they did it for me, and for Michael as well. And, of course, they were well pleased when everyone kept going up to them – Robert Earnshaw, Dermot Browne, Graham Bradley, Chris Pimlott, Kevin Whyte and the rest of them – and having a good chat. It was a great party and we had tremendous fun.

To crown a wonderful season, we won the Racehorse Owners' Association award for the outstanding 'chaser. We were presented with two horse shoes, Monica and Tony getting the other one.

When Silver Buck went back into training following his summer's rest, I was invited over to the stables to see him schooling along with Political Pop. They were both jumping badly and Michael said: 'These are two Cheltenham festival winners and look at them – you wouldn't give me £1,000 for the pair of them, would you?'

Silver Buck started the 1982-83 season by winning Wincanton's Terry Biddlecombe 'Chase for the third time, and Terry made the presentation to us.

They have named a race after Bucket at Wincanton, the Silver Buck Handicap 'Chase and I wanted Master Smudge our old friend from the Sun Alliance 'Chase to win it. But he had too much weight with 12st 4lb and could only finish fifth to Flagstaff. It takes a tremendous amount of effort on the part of the trainer to keep an old favourite like Master Smudge going, season after season.

One of the most spectacular sights I have ever seen in

steeplechasing was in the King George VI 'Chase when Silver Buck, Wayward Lad and Fifty Dollars More jumped the last fence almost in line. I did not think that Wayward Lad was going as well as the other two, but John Francome got enough out of him to win. Silver Buck was not disgraced in finishing third. After all, he was only three-and-a-half lengths away from winning the King George for the third time. Michael was right though in his belief that Silver Buck had not been his true self. When the horse was examined on his return home he was found to have some trouble with his epiglottis.

He was out of action until Market Rasen, less than a fortnight before the Gold Cup, and on the day that he came back I also had Branding Iron running at Haydock. I have a great friend, Annie Binns, who comes racing with me all the time. On this occasion I went to see Silver Buck run at Market Rasen while she went to Haydock, where Branding Iron was taking on Fifty Dollars More, Gaye Chance and Bold Gent in the Timeform Chase. In this way we could compare notes about how each horse ran. It turned out to be nothing but success to report at Market Rasen where Silver Buck completed a treble for Michael after he had won with Sabin du Loir and Last Deal. Annie did not find things going quite as smoothly at Haydock, where Fifty Dollars More beat Branding Iron, while Robert Earnshaw took a nasty tumble when Happy Voyage fell in a novice 'chase.

I used to spend a lot of time with my back turned to the track while a race was on because I get very nervous. Then I decided it was an insult to the horse not to watch him. So I have to do a lot of talking to myself and try to keep a little removed from the scene. It isn't like doing the washing up.

After I had watched Silver Buck win at Market Rasen, a fellow in front of me turned round and stated most emphatically: 'Not as impressive as last year.' I pointed out that Silver Buck had passed the post and won easily under a big weight, but he insisted, 'Not as impressive as last year.' Another fellow, only young, and in jeans and a leather jacket, realising that I was Silver Buck's owner, informed me in no uncertain terms: 'You're the luckiest person on this earth to have a horse like that.'

The chap who had not been impressed with Silver Buck was probably patting himself on the back after the Cheltenham Gold Cup. The horse just crawled home from two fences out after being in the shake-up until that point.

Bucket was a long way behind at the finish but I could not have been more proud of dear old Michael. He had worked so hard to prepare those five horses for the Gold Cup. He is dedication personified, and so very ambitious. I love him.

After the Gold Cup I was in Ladbrokes tent when their representative Mike Dillon said that Julian Wilson wanted to know if Silver Buck would be retiring. I replied that I had not even thought about it, let alone discussed the subject with Michael. Then I heard Julian Wilson say on TV that I was seriously considering retiring the horse, but would not make a decision until I had spoken to Michael.

When it is time for Silver Buck to retire I am sure he will be the one to tell Michael. I am so proud of Bucket. He's given me so much pleasure.

16 Silver Buck's Successor

When Mrs Feather says that 'He's so wonderfully big, so bold, and much too handsome for his own good,' she's not talking about Michael Dickinson, but the horse that could be Silver Buck's successor . . . Branding Iron.

'I was conned by Richard Pitman, William Haggas, who is my middle son, and Michael Dickinson, into buying this extremely expensive gelding from Ian Balding. He was only a baby when we bought him and we had quite a lot of problems with him to begin with. He was supposed to be racing fit, but he was no more fit than I am.

'Branding Iron was going to run within a fortnight of my getting him. But after a lady physiotherapist had looked him over at the stables she told Michael not to run him because he wasn't fit. He is a big horse, and was likely to need plenty of work, and the physiotherapist said that he might have a slight dislocation in his back. And then Branding Iron broke a blood vessel and had to stop work, but it was not a repetitive thing. When he was ready to race he certainly left the opposition for dead in his novice 'chases at Carlisle, Ayr and Kempton, and I think he failed at Cheltenham because the race came too soon after a hard battle at Haydock.'

After showing so much promise in his first campaign over fences it was a bitter disappointment to Mrs Feather and the Dickinsons when Branding Iron was forced to spend the next season on the sidelines.

Michael found that the horse 'had a bit of a leg' and there was no alternative but to rule him out for the 1983-84 campaign.

Mrs Feather, conditioned by several other similar instances

of the uncertainty of racehorse ownership over the years, accepted the situation philosophically.

'It was a great pity that he would not be able to compete in the Embassy Premier 'Chase series, the Final of which would have been his big target. A least, he had shown us in those three wins over fences, and when third in the Timeform 'Chase, that he was a very good horse.

'With the prospect of him being able to return to racing as a seven-year-old, he had time on his side, and there was still every chance of him making it to the top.'

Branding Iron, a chesnut son of Hotfoot, out of Caesars Love, was purchased as a yearling by Ian Balding at the Newmarket Sales. The Kingsclere trainer then passed him on to his godfather, Mr Joe Roebling, who lived in America.

Ian said: 'Sadly, Mr Roebling died, but I wanted to keep Branding Iron because I thought he would make a nice dual purpose horse, so I bought him privately from the estate. I then sold him to Maj. Tony Everett.'

Branding Iron did not race as a two-year-old but pleased his trainer with an encouraging effort in his one outing on the flat as a three-year-old when finishing fifth of twenty behind Saviour in the one mile, three furlongs, Spring Maiden Stakes at Newbury in April.

'He ran with great promise in that race,' said Ian, 'but he was unable to race again in the 1980 season because of a leg injury. We blistered him and after a good rest he was fit to go hurdling in the 1981-82 season.'

Ian was thrilled by Branding Iron's early jumping exploits, the gelding winning novice hurdles at Stratford and Towcester after finishing placed at Newbury and Chepstow. The four-year-old ran up against the unreliable Laska Floko, ridden by Robert Hughes, on one of his more co-operative days in a Newbury novice event and went down by half-a-length, with the third horse, Shady Nook, twenty-five lengths away in a field of eighteen.

Frost and snow wrought havoc with English racing during the following month and the sport was stopped from December 8 until Boxing Day, with the loss of thirty-six cards. The only Boxing Day meeting to survive was Newton Abbot, but racing was possible a couple of days later at Chepstow and Taunton and it was at the Welsh venue that Branding Iron made his second appearance over hurdles.

The Chepstow ground was testing and tailor-made to suit Peaty Sandy, a runaway winner of the Coral Welsh National. I have good reason to remember that winner, having backed him ante-post at 16-1 following his success at Newcastle earlier in the month. He started 3-1 favourite for the Coral contest and romped home ten lengths clear of the runner-up Royal Russe.

Branding Iron did not seem equally at home on going officially described as soft – but looking more like heavy to me – as he took third place behind Silcakey and Pharoah's Own in a Panama Cigar Hurdle Qualifier. The ground was very soft, however, when he opened his winning account in another Qualifier in the same series at Stratford, in February.

Brian Riley, his regular partner, rode him to a two lengths victory over St William, and the combination went on to follow-up at Towcester ten days later. Branding Iron had his Towcester task made much easier when Hasty Storm, who was disputing the lead with him, swerved badly left after the last hurdle and he was able to score by six lengths from John Francome's mount.

Branding Iron's next appearance – and his last for the Balding stable – was in the Panama Cigar Final, at Chepstow, on Easter Monday. On reflection, it is hardly surprising that he failed to win this two miles contest for five-year-olds, although he possibly should have done better than finish a well-beaten fourth to Gaye Brief, Ryeman and Oscar Wilde. He was fourteen lengths adrift of the winner, but even taking that form at face value, it is not bad in the light of Gaye Brief's impressive record since that day.

Just as surely as Silver Buck and Branding Iron were two of the most disappointing performers at the 1983 Cheltenham festival, Gaye Brief had to figure among the big meeting's most brilliant winners. Even Michael Dickinson's Gold Cup five-timer does not overshadow the Waterford Crystal

Champion Hurdle triumph of Mercy Rimell's horse in my fondest memories of the festival. For what it is worth, Gaye Brief gets my vote as the best Champion Hurdle winner over a period of time embracing the victories of such greats as Sir Ken, Persian War, Monksfield and Sea Pigeon. Recalling how well Ryeman had run against Gaye Brief in the previous season's Panama Final, his starting price of 16-1 was generous when he took the Arkle Challenge Trophy some forty minutes before the Champion Hurdle was staged.

However, there were excuses for Branding Iron's below-par efforts in both the Panama Final and the Cheltenham race. He had been absent from racecourse action for nearly two months when he went to Chepstow and Ian Balding maintains: 'He was almost certainly past his best, and may have had the virus on him.

'I thought he would go on to make a good steeplechaser and didn't know whether to sell him or not. But cash is always an incentive, and as I had nothing to work him with, we decided to approach Michael Dickinson and see if he wanted to buy him for steeplechasing.

'It was no surprise to me when he did so well over fences as a novice. But he is a little bit delicate, not a horse who would take a lot of racing, and that is probably why he did not run well at Cheltenham.

'He is tall and rather leggy, probably lacking a bit of substance. Not like the old type of three mile 'chaser. More typical of the flat horse that has become a 'chaser. When he is right again, however, I am sure he will continue to do well.'

The many jumping fans eagerly awaiting Branding Iron's delayed debut for the Dickinson stable had their highest hopes fulfilled when the 2-1 on chance turned in a breathtaking exhibition of foot-perfect fencing. It did not take a potential world-beater to win Carlisle's two miles Walton Novices' 'Chase but the stamp of class was there for the most sceptical to see as Robert Earnshaw's mount cruised home thirty lengths clear of Starmase after leading from the fifth fence.

In post-race interviewing by press correspondents Tony

Dickinson was reluctant to reveal why Branding Iron had missed so many races prior to his debut over fences. 'He has done everything required of him today, and that is what matters,' said Tony, adding that the horse would be in action again at the weekend if none the worse for the Monday run.

The Carlisle race was intended to give Branding Iron some experience over the larger obstacles before a crack at Ayr's valuable West of Scotland Pattern Novices' 'Chase. The Dickinsons had carried off this nice prize in the two previous seasons with Wayward Lad and Seamus O'Flynn. Their new novice star did not let them down in the hat-trick attempt the gelding cruising to another comfortable victory. There was family rivalry in the race, with Branding Iron (15-8) only just shading out Barrier Reef (2-1) – representing Michael Dickinson's brother-in-law, Thomas Tate – from favouritism.

Barrief Reef, assured of staying every yard of the two-and-a-half miles trip, and possibly needing a little further, was soon forcing the pace and maintained the lead until headed by Branding Iron three fences from home. Then Barrier Reef came down, leaving Branding Iron to beat Tudor Folly and Pounentes at his leisure. Thomas Tate admitted that second prize was all he could have hoped for had Barrier Reef remained on his feet. Robert Earnshaw had double cause for celebration, the young jockey having earlier taken his career score to a century on the Peter Easterby-trained Pulse Rate in the Skeldon Handicap Hurdle.

Branding Iron's victory march continued at Kempton, where he had a dozen lengths to spare over The Tsarevich in the two miles Galloway Braes Novices' 'Chase. He would have had more to do but for the challenging Ro's Owen coming to grief at the eleventh fence, but Robert Earnshaw said that his mount was travelling so well that there was never any danger of defeat.

There had been a month between the races at Ayr and Kempton, with the latter outing timed to bring Branding Iron to concert pitch for his big test in Haydock's Timeform 'Chase. The Dickinsons were out for a Timeform double, having won the year before with Wayward Lad, also ridden by Robert Earnshaw. A field of four was a poor turn-out for a contest worth £12,448 to the winner, but Branding Iron was nevertheless thrown in at the deep end against Fifty Dollars More and Gaye Chance. The other runner, Bold Agent, looked outclassed and was priced accordingly at 40-1. Fifty Dollars More had the vital edge in experience, having won the Mackeson Gold Cup and divided Wayward Lad and Silver Buck in the King George. Gaye Chance had started the season by notching two easy wins in novice 'chases. Then he was beaten by Everett at Cheltenham's December meeting, before failing to cope with Combs Ditch in the Lambert and Butler Final, at Ascot. Fifty Dollars More (13-8) was the Haydock favourite, followed by Branding Iron (2-1) and Gaye Chance (9-4) in very tight betting between the 'big three'.

It was predictable that Fifty Dollars More would make the running so that Richard Linley could press home his mount's advantage in experience. Robert Earnshaw kept Branding Iron well in contention with the leader, but Gaye Chance was always struggling to go the pace and it was clear that, barring accidents, Bold Agent would have to be content with fourth prize. Branding Iron was snapping at the heels of Fifty Dollars More from two fences out, but Fred Winter's horse looked to be going the better. Getting the requisite response on the run-in, Richard Linley was able to push his mount home three lengths clear of Branding Iron, who was half-a-length ahead of the staying-on Gaye Chance.

The performance put Branding Iron within something like 10lb of the season's top 'chasers, which was indeed a very high rating for a novice who had only three runs over fences behind him. Whether he would have been equally effective in three mile 'chases is questionable. A form line involving Gaye Chance, Combs Ditch and Bregawn indicated that Branding Iron was worthy of an even higher rating and although this may have flattered the young horse, it did confirm his claims to possessing super-star potential.

Not that there was any evidence of such ability to be derived from his fifth and final performance of the season at the Cheltenham festival. Starting 13-8 favourite for the Arkle Challenge Trophy, he never gave his supporters the slightest hope of collecting. As he trailed in behind Ryeman, it was hard to believe that this was the same Branding Iron who had made his mark so brilliantly when notching a hat-trick, and had gone down so gallantly at Haydock. The 'inquest' verdict was that the hard race at Haydock had taken its toll. Robert Earnshaw subscribed to that opinion and pointed out that Branding Iron was not the only horse to fail dismally at Cheltenham after competing at Haydock Park only ten days before.

'Make no mistake, Branding Iron is an outstanding horse,' asserted Robert, adding, 'he must not have got over his race against Fifty Dollars More, and don't forget that Righthand Man also disappointed in the Sun Alliance 'Chase after winning the Greenall Whitley at Haydock and it was a similar story with a few others. It would be wiser to judge him on his earlier efforts, and Kevin Whyte said after the Carlisle race that I could have nearly pulled him up from the last fence, walked the rest of the way, and still won. He was taking on better opposition at Ayr, but he was always going like a winner. And it was much the same at Kempton. There was never any doubt that he would win. While his best distance was two-and-a-half miles in his first season over fences, I think he will make a top-class three-miler.'

Mrs Feather was well pleased with Branding Iron's initial 'chasing campaign despite the festival flop, and she agreed with Robert that the horse had not recovered from his Haydock exertions.

Rather than dwell dismally on the Cheltenham defeat she characteristically preferred to relate light-heartedly how Ron Barry, after finishing a thirty lengths second to Branding Iron when riding Starmase at Carlisle, had been asked by her friend John Lowthian, 'What do you think of Chris's new horse?' and big Ron had replied: 'It's no use asking me that, I only saw its arse.' After Ron had again finished a well-beaten second to Branding Iron when partnering The Tsarevich at Kempton, Mrs Feather teased: 'You've had another good look at his arse today, Ron.'

The injury to Branding Iron evoked memories for Mrs Feather of an even sadder occasion when a young horse of hers had to be put down.

'I bought an unbroken grey gelding, which I thought was absolutely beautiful. As the fortunes of Yorkshire cricket are followed just as keenly as racing in our household, I decided to call this lovely horse, Headingley. My husband, Robin, is a former captain of the Yorkshire second eleven, and he is now a member of the county committee, and my father was captain of the second team before the war.

'Unfortunately, we were not to have the pleasure of seeing Headingley in action on the racecourse. He was cast in his box on the same day that Silver Buck went lame. Unknown to anyone, he had an abscess, and when he dropped down in his box it burst and septicaemia set in. The leg would not respond to treatment and to our intense regret, we had to have him put down. I only hope that we are more fortunate with a grey that I bought a little while ago and has yet to race. Michael had heard about this one and another Broxted filly, and he left a note on the kitchen table saying: 'Dad, if you have nothing to do today, go down to Wales and look at these fillies. If you like them, bring them back.' Tony thought they were all right, and tipped me off about one of them, saying: "There's a very nice filly here, but I've said nothing to you. Ask to have a look at them and say that you're just interested!"

'Michael had no idea that his father had said that. And when I saw the filly, I fell for her. She is a four-year-old but Michael said it would be sometime before she was ready to run, and he could not be sure whether she would be any good or not. I regard Tony as the greatest judge of horse-flesh. He has a definite flair for judging a horse. Experience may count for a lot, but I think it's a gift. After you have had a horse that has been as successful as Silver Buck, you feel that you need something to follow on. I'll never own another one like him. I think that lightning only strikes once. If Branding Iron is half as good as Bucket, that will do for me!'

17 All Time Greats

Arkle and Golden Miller (named in alphabetical order to allow me to sit on the first fence) would be odds-on to figure as the top two in any list of steeplechasing all-time greats. This pillaging pair, with a combined tally of Gold Cup triumphs putting them one up on the Magnificent Seven, must be rated the Cheltenham rulers supreme. I recall the time that I reminded Tony Dickinson in passing that the mighty Miller, apart from winning the Gold Cup five times, had competed on the Aintree course on seven occasions. After commenting that he could not see Golden Miller's Cheltenham record ever being emulated, Tony added wistfully, 'I wouldn't mind training a few with legs as sound as his must have been.'

Yet, when the man who trained Golden Miller for most of his great victories, Basil Briscoe, first saw the horse he thought he had acquired 'a miserable animal', and one that would never make a racehorse. Briscoe had a high opinion of the horse's dam, Miller's Pride and consequently had bought her son unseen.

Golden Miller did incur a leg injury in an early hunting venture but he recovered fairly quickly and was soon able to race for his new owner, Philip Carr, a patron of Briscoe's stable.

I have no knowledge of whether Golden Miller was prone to 'spook', but he rarely did more than he had to, and the report of his one and only hunting venture, smacks of a Silver Buck style saga, with the horse taking the fences by the roots, failing to keep up with the hounds, and giving Briscoe the worst day's hunting he had ever experienced.

There was something in Golden Miller's conformation that appealed to Philip Carr, however, and he began to look a good judge as the horse improved and filled out. Then Carr unfortunately became ill and Golden Miller was sold to Dorothy Paget for £6,000. That was good money for a steeplechaser in the early 1930s, although no more than loose change to a wealthy woman like Miss Paget. It was a great deal more than Arkle cost when Anne, Duchess of Westminster bought him at the Ballsbridge Sales in Dublin. As Lot No 148, the son of Archive out of Bright Cherry was knocked down to the Duchess – who then became the bay's owner for the rest of his days – for 1,150 gns.

Just like Golden Miller, the gelding was to horrify rather than impress his trainer. That was after arriving at Tom Dreaper's stable in 1961 as a four-year-old. Training maestro Dreaper maintained that 'champions are made in heaven'. Somebody up there must have known something about Arkle that Dreaper did not appreciate at that time. The stable lads were similarly unimpressed and regarded him as the worst of the intake of young horses. They had cause to change their minds somewhat after Arkle, a 20-1 chance, beat his stable companion, Kerforo, in the Bective Hurdle at Navan, in January 1962. He won again at Naas, but lost his next two hurdle races, and had been beaten in a couple of 'bumper' events earlier on.

Nothing outstanding about him as a hurdler, but his career really took off the following season over fences. He had seven outings between October 1962 and May 1963 – five of them in steeplechases – and won them all.

The first glimpse of greatness that he revealed in England came at Cheltenham in November when he hacked up in the Honeybourne 'Chase. From then on it was to be resounding cheers all the way at Cheltenham where he took the Broadway 'Chase the following March.

That was the commencement of an annual majestic March crusade by Arkle at the festival, with victory apparently his divine right. The mighty deeds of the 'perfect gentleman', as his regular partner Pat Taaffe affectionately described him, have of course been well documented. The pair's successes included three Cheltenham Gold Cups, the King George VI 'Chase, two Hennessy Gold Cups, the Whitbread, Irish Grand National and three Leopardstown 'Chases.

Taafe and Arkle were beaten together on only four occasions. Two of those defeats came in what so sadly turned out to be Arkle's final campaign. The first of them served as a sharp reminder to the racing fraternity that there is a limit to the weight that even a 'wonder horse' can concede. At the start of the 1966 season, Arkle could be rated two stones better than most that could be fielded against him. Put another 7lb on top of that, and it added up to his defeat by Stalbridge Colonist, who was receiving all of 35lb from him, in the Hennessy Gold Cup, at Newbury, in November. Well and truly anchored Arkle may have been in the Hennessy but you couldn't keep a mighty horse like him down for long and all the old buoyancy was there as he bounced back to England the following month and cruised to victory in the SGB 'Chase at Ascot.

Arkle's Hennessy reverse came to mind when Silver Buck's top weight burden of 12st 7lb beat him at Catterick in December, 1980. The handicapper had done his sums well enough to give Sunset Cristo a chance, and the lightweight made the most of his 34lb advantage to win by a length. Recalling, too, how Arkle had shrugged off his setback next time out, Silver Buck's defeat did not put me off supporting him when he went to Kempton and won his second King George. Those respective ability-stretching handicap defeats of Arkle and Silver Buck must rank among their most meritorious performances.

I feel that I could not be paying a bigger tribute to Silver Buck than by discussing his career along with that of the legendary Irish horse who captured the imagination of the public in a way that only Red Rum has approached in the jumping world's 'popularity stakes' during the post-war period. A similar compliment was paid to Silver Buck by the *Sporting Life* racing correspondent, George Ennor, in his summing up of prospects for the 1982 King George:

'Some are talking about Silver Buck as "the best chaser since Arkle" and I do not think it is sacrilege to suggest that we may soon be able to talk of the two horses in the same breath.

'Silver Buck's record is of the highest standard and there is evidence to suggest that he is getting better all the time and he has undoubtedly given the lie to the twin theories that he cannot cope with heavy ground and does not stay beyond three miles.

'He must have convinced most of the doubters when he won the Gold Cup at Cheltenham in March.

'This term, Silver Buck followed two virtual walkovers by winning Haydock's Edward Hanmer Chase for the fourth year in a row, trouncing Burrough Hill Lad, Royal Judgement and Gold Cup third, Sunset Cristo, in the process.

'In the 1981 Gold Cup Silver Buck finished third beaten a length and a half and ten by stablemates Little Owl and Night Nurse. He had every chance at the second last, but just did not last home which lent further credence to the belief that he did not stay.

'Well, last year's Gold Cup ruled that idea out of court. Whereas Silver Buck beat Diamond Edge by only four and a half lengths, in 1981 he was more than thirty lengths ahead of that rival last season.'

The Gold Cup victory had revealed the full extent of the repertoire of the horse that stage-managed his own battles. Taking into account that he was found to have a throat problem after the King George, his third to Wayward Lad and Fifty Dollars More was a praiseworthy effort in his attempt to record the first hat-trick in the race.

It was in the King George of 1966 that Arkle's career was so tragically brought to a premature conclusion when he broke a pedal bone in his off fore-leg. The gallant gelding must have been in pain as he struggled to finish a one length second to Dormant, an old rival who had been a distance behind him in the previous year's Kempton contest.

Kept in Kempton stables for several weeks with his injured leg in a 5lb plaster cast, Arkle later recovered to the extent that a possible comeback was talked about, but it was not to be. In 1969, at the age of twelve, he had to be put down, leaving an unparalleled racing record during the post-war era as his legacy.

Every credit to the jump racing fan's 'bible', *Chaseform*, for not missing out at the start of something big. The publication put its subscribers wise to Arkle's potential before he set foot over fences. After winning a handicap hurdle at Gowran Park in October, 1962, *Chaseform* commented: 'A much improved gelding, Arkle now goes chasing and should make an outstanding novice'. Then when he won the Milltown Chase at Leopardstown in February the publication added: 'Arkle again shaped like a future champion.'

It is anyone's guess whether Arkle would have been a match for Golden Miller at Cheltenham, where the Gold prospecting pair blazed such a brilliant glory trail. Golden Miller won a Grand National – and, indeed, pulled off the Gold Cup and National double in the same season – but his overall record in the supreme staying and jumping test they have loosely titled, 'the world's greatest steeplechase', does not put him in the same league as Liverpool specialist, Red Rum. Three victories and two seconds from five successive National attempts, and rarely the hint of a mistake over those treacherous, towering fences when the Aintree turmoil was at its height, must make Red Rum the ruler in a contest which Arkle would almost certainly never have been allowed to enter.

Red Rum went from near the foot of the National handicap right to the top within twelve months, and it is to Crisp's eternal credit that he came within a few tired, tottering strides of thwarting Rummy's first Aintree attempt.

Donald McCain could hardly believe his luck when the 1973 publication of weights for Liverpool's big race revealed Red Rum on the 10st 5lb mark, set to receive weight from his stablemate, Glenkiln. The Southport trainer thought that Glenkiln, although the winner of the William Hill National Trail, on the course, would have been the more leniently assessed of the two. Donald's confidence seemed unbounded during the nerve-tingling days of the National count-down and he asserted about a week before the race: 'Red Rum will win!'

I have always thought that Crisp could have won the Cheltenham Gold Cup during the season that Richard Pitman's mount went so close to conceding 23lb to Red Rum in that never to be forgotten, courageous display of Aintree front running. Crisp had predictably found himself outpaced in the festival's Two-Mile Champion 'Chase when third to Inkslinger and Royal Relief. A couple of days later, Fred Winter and Richard Pitman were pipped in the Gold Cup when Ron Barry got The Dikler home ahead of Pendil in a desperately tight finish.

Red Rum's second Grand National success was achieved at the chief expense of L'Escargot, but the Irish horse was trained specially for Liverpool in the following season, and with a weight advantage of 11lb, he turned the tables convincingly. Ginger McCain readily conceded that Red Rum had been set an impossible task: 'L'Escargot had won the Gold Cup twice and there was something about him. He was a top-class horse!' Only three horses have won the Gold Cup more than twice – Golden Miller, Arkle and the Vincent O'Brien-trained Cottage Rake, who completed a hat-trick in 1950.

When Vincent O'Brien switched his full attention to the flat after sending out the winners of four Gold Cups, three Champion Hurdles and three Grand Nationals, it did not turn out to be very far from his Tipperary yard to even more outstanding success in the classics and other major European flat events.

Cottage Rake was not long out of novice class when he came to Cheltenham in 1948. He obliged at 10-1 after the favourite, Cool Customer, had fallen at the first. A year later, Cool Customer stayed on his feet and had Cottage Rake stretched before going down by two lengths. The Rake's regular partner, Aubrey Brabazon, said that he had never been involved in a harder race, but the hat-trick was obtained easily enough, Cottage Rake winning by ten lengths.

I doubt very much if the competition in those early years after the war was anything like as strong as we have been privileged to see since Arkle's first 'chasing triumph at Cheltenham in 1962. After Arkle and L'Escargot, the Gold Cup was won by Glencarrig Lady, The Dikler and Captain Christy, the latter also a dual victor in the King George. If a medal was struck for the Gold Cup hero who conquered the worst-ever ground conditions it would go to the 1975 winner, Ten Up, who squelched home just before torrential rain stopped racing.

In the 1980s, the Dickinson stable has been notable for housing steeplechasing strength in depth of a standard never likely to be surpassed.

Peter Easterby's stars, Night Nurse, Little Owl and the ill-fated Alverton have also played their part in keeping the North of England to the fore over fences. Sea Pigeon was never asked to jump the larger obstacles but mention of the Easterby team, instantly brings to mind the Champion Hurdle hero and his great battles with Monksfield.

Fred 'Mr Grand National' Winter has been part and parcel of National Hunt racing since I can't remember when . . . preceding Josh Gifford as stable jockey to Capt. Ryan Price. Fred rode two National winners (Kilmore and Sundew) and has trained two (Jay Trump and Anglo), but he is possibly most famous for his association with the much-loved Mandarin and Halloween. Still finding new horizons to conquer, the Lambourn wizard was winning his first Hennessy – either as jockey or trainer – when John Francome took Newbury's brandy prize on Brown Chamberlin. Winter and Francome had struck Gold with Midnight Court at Cheltenham in 1978.

When I asked Michael Dickinson if Arkle would be the best steeplechaser he had ever seen, I thought he seemed a shade grudging in expressing agreement. However, one could understand his being reluctant to concede that there had been one better than his stars, Silver Buck, Gay Spartan, Bregawn, Wayward Lad and Captain John. He was similarly reticent when I quizzed him as to the best 'chaser he had ridden or trained, taking the diplomatic view – as he did before the 1983 Gold Cup – that owners can get upset if you name one to beat another. Before the start of the 1982-83 season, it was no secret that he regarded Silver Buck as his stable's number one. And during the summer of 1983, when he told me: 'Silver Buck can still beat the lot of them,' he was not just referring to the other Harewood team members.

Michael's views on wider aspects of the ever-fascinating subject of all time greats are most emphatic.

Question: How do you think horses such as Golden Miller and Easter Hero would fare against the top steeplechasers of today?

Answer: The old timers wouldn't have a cat in hell's chance!

Question: Why are you so sure that modern horses are superior?

Answer: Jump racing is far more competitive now than in the years before and immediately following the war. Prize money has increased and there are many more runners than there used to be. Today's steeplechasers are so much faster.

For my own part – now that it's time for me to come off the fence – I must confess bias towards the modern horse. Arkle would have to be my selection to beat them all at Cheltenham, but how I would have loved to see Silver Buck taking him on at Haydock, where Mrs Feather's dear old 'Bucket' could not have been more at home if he owned the place.

I shall leave the last word in the all-time greats debate to Silver Buck's trainer.

'You only have to look at those old-time 'chasers to see that they would have had no chance against today's horses. They were like bloody great boats!'

Appendix

Season 1977-78

November, 1977: Ambleside Novices' Hurdle (Div I), Carlisle – UNPLACED
December, 1977: Brompton Amateur Riders' Novices' Hurdle (Div II), Catterick – WON
December, 1977: Philip Cornes Novices' Hurdle Qualifier, Worcester – WON
January, 1978: Nomad Novices' Hurdle (Div II), Leicester – WON
January, 1978: Bristol Novices' Handicap Hurdle, Haydock – WON
January, 1978: Persian War Novices' Hurdle, Chepstow – FOURTH
March, 1978: Sun Alliance Novices' Hurdle, Cheltenham – FOURTH
March, 1978: Maghull Novices' Hurdle, Liverpool – UNPLACED

Season 1978-79

October, 1978: Greystoke Novices' Chase, Teesside – WON
November, 1978: Adam Lindsay Gordon Novices' Chase, Stratford – WON
November, 1978: Embassy Premier Chase Qualifier, Wetherby – WON
December, 1978: Christmas Tree Novices' Chase, Leicester – WON
February, 1979: Fairlawne Chase, Windsor – UNPLACED (brought down)
March, 1979: Embassy Premier Chase Final, Haydock – WON
March, 1979: Sun Alliance Chase, Cheltenham – THIRD

Season 1979-80

November, 1979: Terry Biddlecombe Challenge Trophy Chase, Wincanton – WON
November, 1979: Dewchurch Chase, Hereford – WON
November, 1979: Edward Hanmer Memorial Chase, Haydock – WON
December, 1979: Last Chance Chase, Nottingham – WALK-OVER
December, 1979: King George VI Chase, Kempton – WON
February, 1980: Compton Chase, Newbury – WON
March, 1980: Sean Graham Chase, Hereford – WON

Season 1980-81

November, 1980: ATV Today Chase, Worcester – WON
November, 1980: Whitelaw Gold Cup Chase, Folkestone – WON
November, 1980: Edward Hanmer Memorial Chase, Haydock – WON
December, 1980: W L and Hector Christie Memorial Trophy Handicap Chase, Catterick – SECOND
December, 1980: King George VI Chase, Kempton – WON
February, 1981: Jim Ford Challenge Cup Chase, Wincanton – WON
March, 1981: Tote Cheltenham Gold Cup, Cheltenham – THIRD

Season 1981-82

October, 1981: Terry Biddlecombe Challenge Trophy Chase, Wincanton – WON
November, 1981: Rehearsal Chase, Chepstow – UNPLACED
November, 1981: Edward Hanmer Memorial Chase, Haydock – WON
March, 1982: 'Cox Moore' (sweaters) Handicap Chase, Market Rasen – WON
March, 1982: Tote Cheltenham Gold Cup Chase, Cheltenham – WON

Season 1982-83

October, 1982: Terry Biddlecombe Challenge Trophy Chase, Wincanton – WON
November, 1982: Hawkes Bay Trophy Chase, Stratford – WON
November, 1982: Edward Hanmer Memorial Handicap Chase, Haydock – WON
December, 1982: King George VI Chase, Kempton – THIRD
March, 1983: Budmo Shipping Handicap Chase, Market Rasen – WON
March, 1983: Tote Cheltenham Gold Cup Chase, Cheltenham – FOURTH

Season 1983-84

November, 1983: Whitelaw Gold Cup Chase, Folkestone – WON
November, 1983: Lines Handicap Chase, Market Rasen – WON
December, 1983: Rehearsal Chase, Chepstow – SECOND
January, 1984: Courage Cup Handicap Chase (Qualifier), Cheltenham – WON
January, 1984: John Bull Chase, Wincanton – WON

Total prize earnings (discounting place money): £169,536.90

Index